MW00932237

CHANGING CHANGE

USING LEARNER-CENTERED DESIGN

FROM FAILED INITIATIVES

TO A CHANGE PROCESS THAT CONNECTS, EMPOWERS AND ACTUALLY WORKS.

Graphic Design By:
Charity Allen

**Authored By:
Cale Birk & Charity Allen**

Produced by: PBL Consulting
For questions or information,
please contact PBL Consulting:
www.pblconsulting.org
or info@pblconsulting.org
936 NW 57th St
Seattle, WA 98107

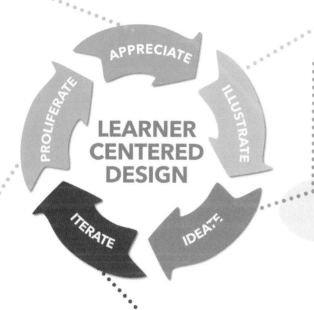

LEARNER CENTERED DESIGN

APPRECIATE · ILLUSTRATE · IDEATE · ITERATE · PROLIFERATE

LET'S CUT TO THE CHASE

WHY SPEND MORE THAN 5 MINS READING THIS?

ARE YOU A SCHOOL LEADER WHO:

Looks at the time on your watch on Monday morning, only to realize that it is Thursday afternoon?

Defines the term "lunch" as "sandwich inhalation?"

Often lays awake the night before faculty meetings, fretting about how you might approach your staff to share a new idea to improve teaching and learning?

Gets frustrated writing school "improvement" plans no one seems to read or follow?

Forces yourself not to guffaw every time you hear the word "budget" because it so often represents a punchline for you and your pals?

Wonders whether professional development really changes practices in classrooms?

Has discovered that you are in fact a direct descendant of a shark because you can never actually stop moving?

Takes your coffee intravenously?

Sincerely loves your school, and truly wants to change the experience for the learners (students, teachers and parents) within it?

If you answered "Yes" to some of these questions, or even just the last one - this book is for you. Making changes in schools today is a challenging proposition, and in the busy lives of school leaders with never-ending initiatives, rising societal demands, shrinking budgets and even less time, finding even a few scant minutes to read a book on change can be a real challenge. We get it.

You're saying this book better be practical. This better give you tools that you can use. And this book needs to reduce the jargon and research from educational mumbo-jumbo to digestible and edible bites for you, and for those you lead. And yes, we heard you, you don't have any more time or money, and the people you've got, well, they are the people you've got. Loud and clear, we hear you.

BY THE COMPLETION OF CHANGING CHANGE YOU WILL...

1 Get deeply connected to problems in your school AND to those who are having them.

2 Become a Design Team leader who can ignite your team's creative juices.

3 Leverage a process to create and proliferate real, battle-tested and lasting solutions to school problems and challenges around implementing new ideas.

4 Prepare to facilitate strategies and techniques during each phase of the process to enable your Design Team to create solutions that are unique and powerful.

5 Ensure you lead a change process that is empowering and unforgettable.

6 Change the experience of change so that it is no longer seen as something that we dread, but rather something that all of us (yes, even those resisters...) actually embrace.

So if you choose to take this journey with us, the Captain has turned on the "fasten seat belt" sign. If you haven't already done so, please stow your carry-on luggage underneath the seat in front of you or in an overhead bin. Fasten your seatbelt and make sure your seat back and tray tables are in their full, upright position. And on behalf of the entire crew, we hope you enjoy your trip FROM where you and your school community are currently at **TO where you really want to go.**

It is truly time to change the experience of change, don't you think? If you still don't believe us, turn the page to see what these really smart people have to say about change and the new role of the leader.

7 REASONS WHY CHANGE IS NEEDED AND WHY WE MUST RETHINK *HOW* WE DO CHANGE...

1 SYSTEMS ARE FAILING KIDS

"Current 'school reform' and 'improvement' efforts are wholly inadequate to the scale of the challenge to prepare young people to live well and sustainably on this planet in the new century... any new paradigm must entail 'a holistic transformational shift towards connected institutions and processes...'" (Hannon, 2009, p. 1)

2 CANNED CHANGE SUCKS

"Prepackaged programs are like prepackaged foods-they go down easy, but provide little sustenance." -Dr. Simon Breakspear, ATA Leadership Conference, 2016

3 MOST CHANGE FAILS

"Most of us know firsthand that change programs fail. We've seen enough 'flavor of the month' programs 'rolled out' from top management to last a lifetime." (Senge, p. 6)

4 EVEN THE BEST IDEAS ARE NOT ENOUGH

It is possible to be "dead right." This is the leader, who has some of the best ideas around, but can't get anyone to buy into them. In fact, the opposite occurs... overwhelming opposition."

-Michael Fullan, in Leading in a Culture of Change

5 SUCCESSFUL ORGS DO CHANGE WELL

Change "...is the defining characteristic of the current era in organizations and... becoming competent at organizational change is a necessary and distinguishing characteristic of successful organizations." (Anderson, 2002, p. 4)

6 COLLABORATIVE INQUIRY INCREASES EFFICACY

"...schools that engage in collaborative inquiry develop a sense of collective efficacy that helps educators reconnect with their original point of passion: ensuring student success." (Langer, 2005, p. 26).

7 LEADERS SHOULD DESIGN LEARNING EXPERIENCES, NOT SOLUTIONS

"Change your approach to strategy and... the leader becomes a context setter, the designer of a learning experience—not an authority figure with solutions. Once the folks at the grassroots realize they own the problem, they also discover that they can help create and own the answer—and they get after it very quickly; very aggressively, and very creatively, with a lot more ideas than the old-style strategic direction could ever have prescribed from headquarters." -Michael Fullan in Leading in a Culture of Change

CHANGE: FROM FAILURE TO FRUITFUL

WHAT COMES TO YOUR MIND WHEN YOU THINK OF CHANGE?

FROM "WHAT IT IS NOW..."

- This too shall pass...
- Fad-ish / Trendy
- Repackaged
- Unrealistic
- We are already doing this...
- Parent Backlash
- Your turn

TO "WHAT IT COULD BE...."

- Meaningful to each participant
- Energizing
- "I'm excited to see this thru"

Pssst...
Yup, that's your cue. You're allowed to dream now. It doesn't have to stay that way.

CHANGE, DONE BETTER

LEARNER-CENTERED DESIGN AT-A-GLANCE

HERE'S YOUR ELEVATOR SPEECH: THE WHAT & THE WHY

Learner-Centered Design (LCD) is a vital tool to meet the challenges being faced in schools and organizations today. Schools are already making invaluable shifts toward becoming learning communities, in which all of its members are learners regardless of title - teacher, leader, student, etc. Thus, *Learner*-Centered Design harnesses the collective capacities of all the *learners* in a learning community to foster continuous improvement. Haven't yet made the transition to becoming a learning community? LCD will act as an accelerator to that end.

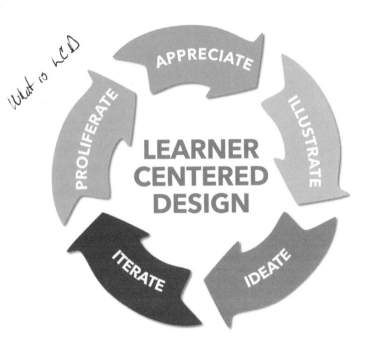

What is LCD

LCD is a powerful extension of participatory action research in which designing and enacting change occurs through a democratic process. LCD has its roots in human-centered design and UX (user-experience), both of which have been used extensively by well-respected organizations such as IDEO and the Hasso Plattner Institute of Design (aka: dSchool) at Stanford University to spark and produce innovative solutions to a wide variety of problems and challenges.

How does it work? In the LCD process, those who experience the problems in our schools, *the Learners themselves* (students, leaders, parents, community members, etc.), are placed at the center of an inclusive, democratic design process in which collaborators ideate, iterate and proliferate powerful solutions - for Learners, by Learners. LCD transforms school leaders into designers and facilitators. It creates teams of curious and empathetic listeners that appreciate the current pain points in our schools, because the teams include those who are experiencing the issues on a daily basis. It involves the co-creation of ideas that utilize the resources we already have in our schools while embracing the day-to-day parameters that surround us. It requires testing and improvement of those ideas in concert with the people that will actually use those ideas. And it involves the creation of high-impact experiences that proliferate measurable solutions from one classroom to all classrooms. From one school to all schools. From within schools to beyond schools. LCD fundamentally redefines the Learner Experience (LX)!

CHANGE, DONE BETTER

THE FIVE PHASES OF LEARNER-CENTERED DESIGN

Greatest Challenges to LCD

APPRECIATE

1

Appreciate: Flatten hierarchies and lead an equitable process to develop a true appreciation of Learner Experiences and empathize with those who are living and breathing them everyday. This often includes interviewing stakeholders, collecting data doing observations and more.

ILLUSTRATE

2

Illustrate: "Sketch" a picture of the end in mind, not in terms of an actual solution, but rather your goals, targets and vision of the yet-to-be-determined solution(s). If we've done this well, we will have an observable list of criteria (what our learners will be saying, doing, producing) and/or indicators of the ideal Learner Experience (LX). You will be able to use these later to measure your own success. Seek feedback from stakeholders before moving on.

IDEATE

3

Ideate: Generate a bank of ideas and possibilities using techniques & strategies to ignite creative juices, challenge our constructs and consider alternatives. Seek inspiration from unexpected sources, existing models, external organizations, other industries, internal expertise, stakeholders, research and more.

ITERATE

4

Iterate: Design, develop and create prototypes of the best ideas and possible solutions in order to improve them. Try and test them in low-stakes settings. Use your goals and criteria from the Illustrate Phase to measure your team's success. Crave feedback and seek it internally and externally. Pivot and adapt until earlier illustrated goals are achieved.

PROLIFERATE

5

Proliferate: Measure success by the quality of the results rather than the completion of the process. Determine best ways to share solutions within a variety of contexts to multiply benefits.

SO...WHAT ABOUT RESISTANCE?

RESISTANCE-O-METER QUIZ

Your teachers would say your mission statement is like...

Our "Educational Red Bull" - It gives our school wings!	✓ A nutritious smoothie - complex, with mysterious ingredients. An acquired taste...	A no-name club soda - generic, flavorless and forgettable.
3	2	1

If you asked your staff members what the vision of the school was, you would get...

An enthusiastic answer and a high five.	✓ A pensive look with an educated and jargon-laden guess.	Crickets...
3	2	1

The number of district and school-based initiatives that you are asking your staff to implement...

Is totally manageable: the staff has them well in hand, and it's smooth sailing ahead.	✓ Seems to be steadily rising; the staff is struggling to keep up, and the ship is feeling the weight.	Rivals the GDP of a small country; the ship is popping rivets and the staff is heading for the lifeboats .
3	2	1

Five minutes prior to the typical staff meetings you lead for your faculty, you...

Rate your vomit-to-excitement ratio as being high: You are getting ready to model the pedagogy and risk-taking for your staff that you want them to do in their classes.	✓ Are wearing a helmet and are looking for a seat in the library with your back-to-the-wall to keep everyone in your line of sight.	Realize that you have a staff meeting in five minutes.
3	2	1

If a staff member shared a problem and it was a song on "Name That Tune" you would...

✓ Listen to the entire song to develop an appreciation for each of its parts - the melody, the refrain and the chorus - before guessing the title.	Listen enough of the melody to make an educated guess.	Nail it on the first note. You've heard lots of songs before, and this one sounds pretty familiar.
3	2	1

Your staff is off task during an inservice with a speaker you brought in. In your head, you are...

✓ Velma from Scooby Doo: This is a mystery, and I need to figure out why people aren't picking up what this dude is throwing down...	The Flash: Thoughts flicker in and out. PD is important, but yes, there are a few fires burning back at the ranch.	The Incredible Hulk: Cue muscle-bound tantrum, flipping cars in a pair of ripped jeans. This is an outrage! And heads will roll...
3	2	1

If your score is between:

15-18	10-14	6-9
Congratulations! Your readiness for change is higher than most!	You're skating on thin ice...	You're creating a dangerous hot-bed of resistance...

SO...WHAT ABOUT RESISTANCE?

LEADERSHIP OR ACCIDENTAL DICTATORSHIP?

JUST GET EVERYBODY "ON BOARD," RIGHT...?

We get it.

ENDLESS INITIATIVES

DIGITAL HYPER-SATURATION

SHRINKING BUDGETS

ATTACK HELICOPTER PARENTS

RISING SOCIETAL DEMANDS

As we rapidly move through the first quarter of the 21st century, most would agree that "change" seems to be one of the few conversational constants in our schools across North America. But real, powerful change is rare. Why is that?

Change, as a constant, is the **only** common pattern in the dozens of schools-that-work that we've seen, studied and supported around the nation and world. They have achieved **a homeostasis of continuous improvement.** Thus, their constant *is change*. They change purposefully to improve thinking, practice, Learner Experiences and results. However, if we want change to be the new constant, and change is horribly unpleasant, then let's face it, no one will want to do it.

So, let's reframe our approach to change. Each of us "knows" that the real power of a leader is not in telling, managing or dictating a solution. And yet, too often change looks like making decisions behind closed doors, creating solutions before having deeply understood the problem and implementing initiatives without involving those who will be affected by them. Ouch.

That's a recipe for a dish called: **"Dictatorship à la whoops..."**

Inadvertently, we become the dictators that we don't want to be and in the process, we don't "deal with" resistance, **we actually create resistance!** Leaders must acknowledge that the experience of change matters, and the new role of the leader is framing and leading a better change experience - one that is both effective and enjoyable (aka: High LX.)

But how do we do it?
How do we "change" change?
Stick with us, there is a better way...

FROM THIS...TO THAT...

BUT WHAT EXACTLY?

FROM ·············▶ **TO**

STAFF MEETINGS	**FROM** obligatory meetings that we dread	**TO** powerful collaborative experiences that we crave
PROFESSIONAL DEVELOPMENT	**FROM** something that is done **to** educators	**TO** powerful learning and modeling that is done **with, for and by** educators
SCHOOL AND DISTRICT IMPROVEMENT PLANS	**FROM** pieces of paper that are created by few, read by even fewer and loved by nearly no one	**TO** organic processes evolving in ways that connect us with one another and inspire us to action
THE SCHOOL EXPERIENCE	**FROM** distant hopes about what it could be	**TO** the daily truth lived by us all

"What is needed from a leadership perspective are new forms of improvisational expertise, a kind of process expertise that knows prudently how to experiment with never-been-tried-before relationships, means of communication, and ways of interacting that will help people develop solutions that build upon and surpass the wisdom of today's experts."

– The Practice of Adaptive Leadership (Heifetz, 2009, p2)

So that we can model how to inspire solutions for all of our learners in classrooms, schools, districts, communities and beyond.

A BETTER PATH

BUT, HOW? HOW DO WE "CHANGE" CHANGE?

Bottom line: If we want to change the experience of change, we can no longer do change TO people. Rather than saying: "We need to improve student engagement, and here's how," we must instead design and lead an inclusive process from which solutions can emerge. The leader's real power is not in telling, solving, managing or dictating solutions. Rather, their real power is in reframing and leading *how we do change*. If that experience of change is enjoyable, empowering and effective, then people will want to do it. Thus, the new role of the leader is to design powerful change experiences.

Ahem...that would be LCD:

ILLUSTRATE:
We paint a picture (*figuratively*) of the ideal to distill down our actual goals.

IDEATE:
We ignite the creative juices to uncover unique solutions.

APPRECIATE:
We flatten hierarchies and use our existing expertise to deepen our understanding of the problem and empathize with those affected by it.

ITERATE:
We create, prototype, crave feedback and pivot until we get the types of learning experiences we want.

PROLIFERATE:
We measure our success by the quality of our results rather than the completion of the process. Then, we share them out in different contexts.

Just remember, while you're a skilled, experienced and charismatic leader, that's not enough. A system that is dependent on a single person's vision, skill, charisma or creative mind is one job-transfer away from disaster. LCD is a not a solution created or implemented by one person, it is a **process** with the goal of democratizing school innovation and professional learning. Ongoing use of LCD leads to continuous improvement of thinking, practice, LX and results.

So, I have to surrender control... What if they don't do it right?

They don't want control except on final [handwritten note]

Your real safety is in the structure of the process itself. The quality of process will impact the quality of results. In other words, you must do the process well - target a problem, frame a question, select a team, connect your team, set clear parameters, lead each phase of LCD as well as provide resources, support and encouragement along the way. All of that sounds like a lot, but it's precisely what this book will help you do, step-by-step.

Your LCD Pals — Contact

100% 10:12 AM

> So look, it's time for us to have a chat. Change staff meetings and District Plans? That's not possible. No way.

Way.

> Those are moonshot goals. Kinda idealistic, wouldn't you say?

Sure, challenge accepted.

> I don't have any more time or money. I can't do that.

OK, then don't.

> Don't what?

Just tell them in advance.

> What do you mean? Tell who?

Just tell your school community in advance, before they send their kids to your school.

> Tell them what?

That you can't do any of those things. Then they can take their kids somewhere else.

> Well, I want to. I just don't see how I CAN do it.

You can't.

> What do you mean I can't?

YOU can't. You can't do it by yourself. NO ONE can do these things by themselves. That's why change is so hard.

> So, you're saying I don't have to do all of this by myself?

Precisely. You will do it with people in your school. And people in your community.

> But how can they help? They don't understand the problem.

If you ask them, you might find that YOU don't understand the problem.

 Send

100% 10:12 AM **Your LCD Pals** Contact

But talking to them will take time!

A bit, yup.

Do you like dealing with complaints?

No.

Do complaints take up a lot of your time?

Well...I guess so, yes.

If you could turn those who complain into people who collaborate, would that be ok?

Well, yeah. But some of them are really resistant.

Yup. And just imagine how much more resistant they will be when you exclude them again. Most people are pretty nice when you show them you actually want to listen to them.

This helps you change things like staff meetings and school plans AND even change resisters into collaborators. But that's not all...

There's more? What else?

We're not telling.

What? Why won't you tell me?

Have you seen The Shawshank Redemption?

No! I heard that movie is awesome!

At the end of the movie, the main character escapes from prison and lives happily ever after on a beach in Mexico.

Come on! Why would you tell me how it ends? Now I don't even have to see the movie. Sheesh, that wasn't very nice.

Sigh.

So before you toss this book aside, if there were a process that could help you make these sorts of changes, would it be worth reading about? If you could learn a method to embrace change so you could change the EXPERIENCE of change, would it be worth your while? Read on, dear friend. Read on.

Hard sell

Send

UX - UNLOCKING OPPORTUNITY

AND WHO CARES?

BUT WHAT IS THIS WHOLE "EXPERIENCE" THING ANYWAY?

Have you ever gotten a new piece of technology and within 1.5 minutes, you feel ready to throw it at the wall? **That's low UX** (user-experience.) On the flip-side, imagine 3 minutes of exploring another piece of new technology, and you suddenly declare: "This is awesome, it just makes sense!" That's high UX. How about trying to unsubscribe for the third time to an email list you never signed up for after receiving the seventh unwanted email in just two weeks? Annoying. **Low UX.** How about an email that makes you laugh-out-loud and leaves you wanting more? High UX. And, it should be the standard.

─────────────────────── UX matters. ───────────────────────

> Jot down a positive user interaction or experience that you have had in the past few months....

Complimentary email f/ parent (mk)

TM slide f/ today

Perhaps one positive UX was at a restaurant, where you had an exceptional meal and an energetic, engaging server. Maybe it was when your car needed repairs, and the mechanic not only managed to save you a great deal of money on a repair by truly digging into the problem, he gave you a ride to work because your vehicle was going to take two hours longer than expected. Or maybe you were assembling a ceiling fan in your kitchen, and the directions were laid out in a manner that was so clear, intuitive and helpful that when you were finished, you thought: "Wow. That was really easy!" You just had a great "user-experience!"

While the concept of user-experience can trace its roots to interactions between man and machine - in industrial design and systems - the term "user-experience" (or UX) has become a more commonly applied term thanks to the work of Don Norman when he was the Vice President of the Advanced Technology Group at Apple. Norman is the author of numerous books on design, most notably The Design of Everyday Things, and is an expert in cognitive science and usability engineering. Norman and Jakob Nielsen define user-experience as something that "encompasses all aspects of the end-user's interaction with the company, its services, and its products". They describe an exemplary user-experience as one that: "meets the exact needs of the customer, without fuss or bother"

In the business world, creating a rich and positive UX for a customers and clients is essential for successful enterprises. Yet, how might we apply this concept to our schools?

LX - YOUR NEW MASTER KEY

AND WHY YOU SHOULD CARE

YOUR SCHOOL'S PERFORMANCE WILL NEVER EXCEED IT'S OWN LX.

So what's the quality of "the experience of school" for:

Our Students?   **Our Educators?**   **Our Parents?**

In our schools we have virtually unlimited and direct access to our "users" *(but from now on, let's call them "Learners," "Users" sounds so cold!)* Learner can refer to anyone participating in our learning communities - students, educators, parents and more. Voilà: **LX - for "Learner Experience."**

Learners are in front of us in our classrooms, in the staff room, and in the parking lot of our schools each day. Yet, how often do we ask Learners, who are experiencing our schools, about their experiences?

If we don't get to know the current LX, as perceived by our Learners, then it should come as little surprise to us, as school leaders, to know that we are likely to disenfranchise a significant portion of our school community whether we maintain the status quo OR whether we decide to change something. In either case, we cause resistance! **#oops.**

#oops. Making changes without developing a deep understanding of the experiences at our schools and those who are having those experiences is simply "change for the sake of change." No wonder change is so hard.

LOW LX BEST CASE SCENARIO:	HIGH LX BEST CASE SCENARIO:
If you asked a **student**: "I got my A. Not sure what I'm supposed to do now..."	If you asked a student: "I can make a difference."
If you asked a **parent**: "Whatever. My kid got into Stanford."	If you asked a parent: "You should see what they did at PT interviews--amazing! Oh, and by the way, my kid got into Stanford!"
If you asked a **community member**: "I have no idea what kids learn these days."	If you asked a community member: "That school makes our community better. Period."
If you asked **alumni**: "I played the game of school. But, now I have to make sense of the real world."	If you asked alumni: "That school changed my life. My kids will go there one day. "

LX AT YOUR SCHOOL

A QUESTION OF PERSPECTIVES

LET'S DO A QUICK ACTIVITY TOGETHER

Think of Learning Experiences at your school that have *(or should have)* a significant impact on Learners. E.g. Staff meetings, conferences, etc.

Step One

List words that would describe HIGH LX (Learning Experience)

Hint:
Personalized
Engaging

satisfying
enjoyable
productive

Step Two

Repeat Step One, except choose an LX at your school and list words that describe the LX you've named below.

STEP

Learning Experience at your school: PSSA Results

Step Three

Consider those who have this LX at your school. Predict and list the words they might use to describe this experience.

frustrating
discouraging
hopeless

We collect and use feedback from Learners on this. ☐ Yup ☐ Nope

Pssst...You can pick and name the LXs here & here

What might happen if we actually asked our Learners?

Step Four

Repeat Step Two, except choose and write another LX below.

Learning Experience at your school:

_____

Step Five

Repeat Step Three, except just list words the Learners themselves would use to describe this 2nd LX.

lkhing

boring
not relevant

We collect and use feedback from Learners on this. ☐ Yup ☐ Nope

SHOW ME THE MONEY

LCD PROCESS & RESULTS FOR PT CONFERENCES

TARGETED LX

The Learning Experience (LX) to be addressed. Current perceptions of this LX.

LX: Parent-Teacher (PT) Interviews

CURRENT PERCEPTIONS OF LX: PT Conferences are poorly attended, misunderstood and perceived, at best, as obligatory by parents - the very people they are intended for...

FOCUSING QUESTION

The "minute-to-get-it" call to action...

How might we transform PT Interviews for our busy parents into nights they always want to come to and never want to leave?

DESIGN TEAM

Assembling & connecting a strategic team.

Ruth (Principal), Manpreet (student), Joan (Art Teacher), James (Parent Booster Club President) Kesha (PAC chair), Garth (Band Teacher), Melinda (Head Clerical), Shawna (Local events coordinator)

▶ APPRECIATE   Empathizing about current state of LX.

PT Interview stats from last three years and focus group style interviews with (1) Parents that DO & DO NOT come (2) Parents that attend other events and (3) Community partners that host big events

▶ ILLUSTRATE   Crafting a vision, while avoiding ideation.

To begin visioning (what we should be able to observe our Learners saying and doing during this LX) we will explore these questions: What are the events our parents would never miss? How could we make our busy parents feel special?

LEARNER CENTERED DESIGN

APPRECIATE · ILLUSTRATE · IDEATE · ITERATE · PROLIFERATE

▶ IDEATE   Igniting creativity to generate tons of ideas.

What are events that you never miss? Why not? What and how do you want to hear about when it comes to your student's progress? What would make PT nights better? Worse? What events bring our whole community out? Where are the nights where parents feel extra special about their children, and extra special about themselves? How might we take one of those "all-in" events and combine it?

▶ ITERATE   Trying, testing & improving.

Test our ideas out at a staff lunch and PTA meeting. Focus group.

▶ PROLIFERATE   Spreading solutions in best way(s).

Videos, testimonials, pictures, community press, invite feeder school principals.

How PT Interviews Became "A Night On The Town" For Parents

SAMPLE LCD PROCESSES AND THEIR RESULTS...

TARGETED LX

The Learning Experience (LX) to be addressed. Current perceptions of this LX.

LX: Collaboration Time

CURRENT PERCEPTIONS OF LX: Collaboration time seems rushed, infrequent, lacks purpose and is generally not valued. Students often treat the associated self-directed time as free time.

FOCUSING QUESTION

The "minute-to-get-it" call to action...

How might we create meaningful collaborative opportunities for our people to improve the lives of our Learners?

DESIGN TEAM

Assembling & connecting a strategic team.

Amanda (Head of Science & Math), Taj (9th Grader), Sherri (11th Grader), David (parent of 10th Grader), Harp (Industrial Ed. Teacher), Seema (Principal), Lisa (Humanities teacher), Micheline (Business Ed. Teacher & Teacher Association Rep.)

▶ APPRECIATE
Empathizing about current state of LX.

Processes to understand current LX for busy students, parents and teachers? We know our school community doesn't always respond to surveys, so what can we use to understand those who are having the issue?

▶ ILLUSTRATE
Crafting a vision, while avoiding ideation.

To begin visioning (what we should be able to observe our Learners saying and doing during this LX) we will explore these questions: Where would be find examples of successful teams who make a difference and how are they so successful?

LEARNER CENTERED DESIGN

APPRECIATE · ILLUSTRATE · IDEATE · ITERATE · PROLIFERATE

▶ IDEATE
Igniting creativity to generate tons of ideas.

Which schools have achieved the deepest level of practice with teacher collaboration, serving students equitably and interventions for struggling kiddos? What are other countries doing? Finland? What are the most successful industry players doing in terms of creatively supporting workplace learning and closing performance gaps?

▶ PROLIFERATE
Spreading solutions in best way(s)

Team brainstorming session to investigate best ways to proliferate. Early Ideas include: (1) Edcamp-style experience & modeling of various protocols and approaches and (2) sharing at District's Professional Learning Day. as well as possible conference presentation proposals.

▶ ITERATE
Trying, testing & improving

Small groups of teachers, and small groups of students. Action research. Specific, descriptive, non-judgemental observations. Input from stakeholders. Check-in against vision language from Illustrate Phase.

How Teacher Collaboration Time Became "Quest Block" For Teachers And Students

SAMPLE LCD PROCESSES AND THEIR RESULTS...

TARGETED LX

The Learning Experience (LX) to be addressed. Current perceptions of this LX.

LX: Student Course Selection Process

Current Perceptions of LX: Student course selection process is boring, unappealing and uninspiring. Enrollment in electives has dropped significantly.

FOCUSING QUESTION

The "minute-to-get-it" call to action...

How might we create a positive and unforgettable experience to showcase the programs in our school?

DESIGN TEAM

Assembling & connecting a strategic team.

Rachel (11th grader), Kai (Senior), Mr. Stone (Father of 11th Grader, & Travel Agent), Amara (Alumni, now at university), Shaundra (Media Arts teacher), Mr. Hernandez (Principal)

▶ APPRECIATE   Empathizing about current state of LX.

Focus Group: Bring a cross section of students and parents together to go through the course selection process, given the current info available. Interviews: with alumni and parents, to determine if the course selection material was accurate in helping them with admission to college

LEARNER CENTERED DESIGN

PROLIFERATE • APPRECIATE • ILLUSTRATE • IDEATE • ITERATE

▶ ILLUSTRATE   Crafting a vision, while avoiding ideation.

When you are curious about learning something new, where do you go to find information? If you are curious about a course, what would you want to know? Who would you believe? Where can we look for inspiration and possibilities?

▶ IDEATE   Igniting creativity to generate tons of ideas.

What are other examples of goods or services where people want to make informed decisions? What are the most inspiring course catalogs in education and what makes them extraordinary?

▶ ITERATE   Trying, testing & improving.

Focus groups: small groups of students, parents and alumni

▶ PROLIFERATE   Spreading solutions in best way(s).

Archive process and product with photos, interviews, and finally the posted Course Selection Tour Guide.

How School Course Descriptions Became a Travel Brochure...

SAMPLE LCD PROCESSES AND THEIR RESULTS...

TARGETED LX

The Learning Experience (LX) to be addressed. Current perceptions of this LX.

LX: Quality of day-to-day learning

CURRENT PERCEPTIONS OF LX:
Students are not engaged in learning, and for that matter, neither are teachers.

FOCUSING QUESTION

The "minute-to-get-it" call to action.

How can we all fall back in love with learning again?

DESIGN TEAM

Assembling & connecting a strategic team.

Students, Parents, Teachers from Several Grade Levels, Several Teachers, Alumni, Administration

▶ APPRECIATE Empathizing about current state of LX.

Classroom observations, teach/co-teach teachers' classes, shadow-a-student for a day, interviews of teachers, parents & students, observe planning time. What exactly are we trying to help students learn? How is that going?

▶ ILLUSTRATE Crafting a vision, while avoiding ideation.

To begin visioning (what we should be able to observe our Learners saying and doing during this LX) we will explore these questions: What do our most memorable and enjoyable learning experiences have in common?

LEARNER CENTERED DESIGN

APPRECIATE · ILLUSTRATE · IDEATE · ITERATE · PROLIFERATE

▶ IDEATE Igniting creativity to generate tons of ideas.

What are Learners saying and doing at the most successful schools in the world? What are the most successful industry players doing in terms of creatively supporting workplace learning? Use "Word Listing" brainstorming method.

▶ PROLIFERATE Spreading solutions in best way(s).

Participating teachers reflect upon changes in practice and in students. What went well and not so well in a blog or even a presentation at a faculty meeting. Maybe teachers then do demo lessons for other teachers to familiarize other teachers with the strategies that they find to be successful. I'm thinking a project slice type thing here.

▶ ITERATE Trying, testing & improving.

Small groups of teachers who would like to participate. Action Research.

How This Staff Dove Into Deeper Learning, On Their Own...

TARGET A PROBLEM

YOU WILL HAVE NAILED THIS IF...

SO WHERE DO WE START? WHICH EXPERIENCES DO WE FOCUS ON?

Think: The three little bears.... Not too hot, not too cold...just right.

While there are dozens of face-to-face and digital experiences taking place each day, we must carefully narrow our focus. Start with potentially "high-impact" areas. In other words - if you solve "these problems," you'll have a high likelihood of significantly and positively impacting the culture and/or learning environments of your school. Just think, if the problem you select was replaced by experiences that were exceptionally positive, that "delighted" Learners, then the learning environment could substantially change for the better.

For example, while ensuring that our school grounds are neat and free of litter is important, it is unlikely that having a litter-free playground will result in a **dramatic** change to the learning in classrooms. And although having a litter-free school property might be a challenge that would benefit from LCD at some point, we must prioritize the learning first.

YOUR TASK: Target a problem that will significantly and positively impact learners in your school and that will create an opportunity for an early success with your Design Team. i.e. It's not TOO hard, as your first-go-at-this...

Math

YOU WILL HAVE NAILED THIS STEP IF....

WHAT YOU SHOULD BE ABLE TO SAY	WHY YOU SHOULD BE ABLE TO SAY IT
You envision yourself being an educational "Rocky" - punching hanging sides of beef and looking for a lengthy flight of stairs to climb.	Your enthusiasm about the idea of connecting to the problem and the people who are having it will be contagious.
After telling your staff what you're going to work on, a teacher asks you for a moment of your time and then gives you a 12-second, ear-to-shoulder hug, while saying, "thank you, thank you."	Your targeted problem is perceived as worth solving by your learners. It's a problem that your school community needs to solve, wants to solve and will truly make a difference.
After everyone has left the meeting where you just did "the big reveal" of the target problem, you break into a cold sweat, clutch your hair and shriek, "what have I done..!?"	This angst is natural in the face of a problem you don't actually know how to solve. It would be scarier if you were gleefully skipping and whistling with a solution already in your mind that you were simply delaying imposing.

WHICH PROBLEM SHOULD I TACKLE FIRST?

DECISIONS, DECISIONS...

Time to choose an element of the LX in your school that could use an overhaul. But, how to choose? Trying using this matrix:

FACTORS FOR CONSIDERATION

TARGET LX	Potential Impact on Teaching & Learning 1: Low 2: Medium 3: High	Potential Impact on Culture & Tone 1: Low 2: Medium 3: High	You are open to changing this... 1: Not really 2: Indifferent 3: Absolutely	This LX element is urgent 1: Not really 2: Neutral 3: Definitely	Total Score The higher the score the better!
Faculty Meetings	1	2	2	1	6
Your School Vision for Student Learning	2	2	2	2	8
Team & Collaboration Time for Teachers	3	3	3	3	12
Professional Learning	2	2	3	2	9
Parent Interface	2	1	3	2	8
Community Interface	1	2	2	1	6
Continuous Improvement Processes	3	2	3	3	11

THE PROBLEM THAT I PLAN TO TARGET WITH LCD AND WHY:

Continuous Improvement

CRAFT A FOCUSING QUESTION

YOU WILL HAVE NAILED THIS STEP IF...

WHAT'S STARBUCKS MISSION STATEMENT? MAKE GREAT COFFEE, RIGHT?

Wrong. Their mission statement is not: "Make Great Coffee." It's actually: "To inspire and nurture the human spirit – one person, one cup and one neighborhood at a time." (Starbucks, 2017)

If our questions are as mundane, indifferent and misdirected as: "What's the best way to cover content?" and "How can we improve student achievement on standardized tests?" then we actually have a bigger problem to solve.

YOUR TASK: Frame a Focusing Question that inspires, calls others to action and shines a light in a direction worth heading.

YOU WILL HAVE NAILED THIS STEP IF....

WHAT YOU SHOULD BE ABLE TO SAY	WHY YOU SHOULD BE ABLE TO SAY IT
When you try to find an answer to your focusing question with Google, the search returns a single link that says "OK, you got us on that one."	Great news, if you can't Google an answer to your problem, you have probably selected an LCD-worthy problem.
When you ask your question to colleagues, they start to answer, but quickly stop and say "Wait, I know who else could help us figure this out!"	Your question should invite multiple perspectives from a diverse and eclectic group of thinkers.
If you were to ask Arsenio Hall your question, he would nod at you and say "That's one of those things that makes you go 'Hmmmmmm....'"	Well done, your question meets the "minute-to-get-it, but a lifetime-to-master" criteria.
Your cell rings in the middle of the night and it's one of your Design Team members, saying, "So, I've been thinking about that question…"	Your question is so compelling that there's a buzz in the air and your people are voluntarily kicking around ideas.

"Why are we doing things the way we've been doing them all along? What if we tried a whole new approach? That, to me, is a beautiful question." - Warren Berger in Education Week Teacher

CRAFT A FOCUSING QUESTION

NOT ALL QUESTIONS ARE CREATED EQUAL

WHICH OF THESE MIGHT INSPIRE WILD AND CRAZY THOUGHTS & MULTIPLE SOLUTIONS?

ROUND ONE - If you can make speeding tickets interesting...

OPTION A		OPTION B		YOUR IDEA HERE...
How do we get people to stop speeding in our neighbourhood?	VS	How might we make our streets safe places where parents want their kids to play?	→	*signs*

ROUND TWO - But could you can bring intrigue to toasters....?

OPTION A		OPTION B		YOUR IDEA HERE...
"How do we make a better toaster?"	VS	"How might we inspire people to tell others about their breakfast?"	→	*better food choices*

ROUND THREE - Well how about the school context?

OPTION A		OPTION B		YOUR IDEA HERE...
"How can we make staff meetings more effective?"	VS	"How might we create learning experiences that everyone wants to come to and no one wants to leave?"	→	*participants deliver*

ROUND FOUR - Ok, gimme another one.

OPTION A		OPTION B		YOUR IDEA HERE...
"How do we make better parent teacher conferences?"	VS	"What can we learn from events at our school that parents never want to miss to improve our conferences?"	→	*student perf.*

ROUND FIVE - It's all about shifting the frame!

OPTION A		OPTION B		YOUR IDEA HERE...
"How do we improve the perception of our school?"	VS	How might our school do something important for our community?	→	*service*

ASSEMBLE A DESIGN TEAM

YOU WILL HAVE NAILED THIS STEP IF...

"YOU HAVE A BIOLOGIST ON YOUR TEAM, WHY WOULD YOU DO THAT?"

The famous design firm IDEO set the standard for diverse teaming decades ago with their approach that looked a bit like: "Well sure, why not..?" Now, more and more, visionaries and realists in all types of industries are seeing the value of seemingly-unexpected-pairings when forming powerful teams. One winning example is in the field of engineering where industry experts and newbies alike see the enormous value of finding inspiration from nature to solve tough engineering problems. This has led to the entire domain of Biomimicry, defined by Janine Benyus - the founder of the Biomimicry Institute - as: "Sustainable Innovation Inspired by Nature." That means a team of engineers might collaborate with biologists to investigate new ways to synthesize concrete from CO_2 in the air - like how sea shells form, except in seawater - or create color from nano-structures that only reflect a certain wavelength of light, instead of using toxic chemical pigments - like the wings of a butterfly that are free of any pigments and produce color by structure-alone.

YOUR TASK: Assemble a wildly diverse, perhaps unexpected and definitely strategic Design Team, with the potential to co-opt resisters.

YOU WILL HAVE NAILED THIS STEP IF....

WHAT YOU SHOULD BE ABLE TO SAY	WHY YOU SHOULD BE ABLE TO SAY IT
You're NOT referring to your team as: "the peanut gallery."	The team is not a-necessary-evil. Your genuine intention is to harness their collective capacities.
When you tell staff who the members of the team will be, they do a double-take, begin to say something, stop, hold up a finger, start to nod, and say "Hmmm, yes that's a good team."	There should be people on your team who have not been tagged for this type of work before, but have perspectives that will really help the group.
People may be wondering if you have just watched Forrest Gump when they look at your team: "Life is like a box of chocolates. You never know what you're going to get."	Unique solutions call for unique teams with diverse combinations of skills, perspectives and personalities.
"They may be a resister... But, if we want to understand the problem, we need to understand everyone who is having it."	We need to re-think "resistance." If we continue to ignore it or pretend it's not there, well...as Dr. Phil would say: "How's that working for you?"

DISRUPT YOUR ROUTINES

CHANGE THE WAY YOU THINK ABOUT TEAMING

In his book "Liminal Thinking," Dave Gray talks about creating the change you want by changing the way you think:

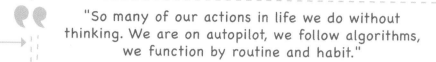

> "So many of our actions in life we do without thinking. We are on autopilot, we follow algorithms, we function by routine and habit."

As school leaders, we indeed can sometimes become algorithmic in our approach to solving problems when we follow a tried-and-true pattern that seems to work for us. Typically, many of us have our "go-to" people on staff - the people that are always up for trying something new and who love a juicy problem to solve. *I don't have go-to's*

(If you close your eyes, you can probably envision who those people might be - it's ok, we all have them!)

We can become very reliant on this hard-working group--they are usually easy to work with, fun and have a "we can do this" attitude that is infectious and makes the problem-solving process more enjoyable. Yet as leaders, we have to be cautious about 'going to the well' too often.

Utilizing the same team to work through complex issues can be problematic for several of reasons:

- The challenge may require skills that your "go-to" gang may not have
- We can become complacent and stagnant in the group - fresh perspectives can be helpful
- We can build resentment and resistance among others who aren't part of the 'in' crowd
- We fail to distribute leadership and build the problem-solving capacity of others
- "Go-to" people are just people. They need a break too!

At the Business Innovation Factory (BIF) Summit in Rhode Island, founder and author Saul Kaplan encourages: "random collisions of unusual suspects." His experience points to the fact that we will increase the possibility of creating unique ideas and different solutions when we bring diverse and eclectic groups of thinkers together who might not have had the opportunity to think with each other.

KEY POINT: By assembling a team that surprises and delights, we can increase our chances in coming up with a solution that does the same.

So, how do we enable this random collision of unusual suspects in our schools? What is the recipe for a team that can create new and unique ideas to solve our school's problems? Flip to find out.

ASSEMBLE A DESIGN TEAM

WHO SHOULD I PUT ON MY TEAM?

BE ON THE LOOKOUT FOR UNEXPECTED EXPERTS

(handwritten margin notes: Behav. Cohort — Ken K.; Prompt for other students; Consideration of ok for consen.; LIM; Family Mission Stmt; PTO-training)

WHO TO INCLUDE

(1) Internal and external stakeholders
(e.g. teachers, parents, alumni, etc.),
(2) high performers from multiple levels
in your school and (3) unexpected experts,
all with valuable skill sets and
strong desires to address the problem.

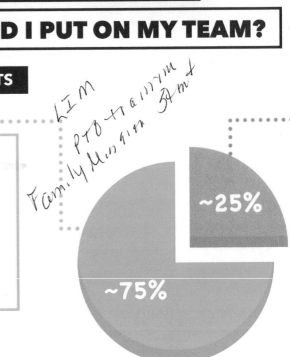

~25%

~75%

WHY WOULD I DO THAT?

Teams often have a disproportionate number of members who are "on-board." This critical mass of motivated and capable individuals are an important asset in its own right and importantly they can also balance potential push-back from "resisters."

Perhaps just as important is the diversity of skill sets and opinions that team members bring to the table! If the team bus breaks down on the side of the highway, while it's great to have people that are highly motivated to fix the engine, it's even better when one of them happens to be a mechanic - even if he is grumpy from time to time. Those skill sets bring important lens through which to look at your targeted problem. Plus, you never know when team members hidden talents might come in handy!

This underscores why it is so important for LCD leaders to enable "the random collisions of unusual suspects" as Saul Kaplan suggests. If we always bring together the same people to try to change the Learning Experiences in our school, we will never surface those "unexpected experts" among us in our own school community!

> "Innovation comes from the edges, so it comes as no surprise that
> **innovators are found in the margins.**
> They are the misfits among us, the ones who see & do things differently."
> ERIK HERSMAN, Co-founder, Qatar Computing Research Institute

SO, WHAT ABOUT THOSE RESISTERS?

A HEALTHY SYSTEM WELCOMES A CHALLENGE.

WHO TO INCLUDE

"Resisters" who (1) are "thought leaders" for other "resisters" (aka: taste-makers), who (2) are motivated by autonomy and who (3) don't have any significant performance issues.

WHY WOULD I DO THAT?

"Resister" Rethink: Have you ever challenged the status quo? Can you think of a time when you may have been considered a "resister?"

Why did you resist? You probably had a lot of good reasons. In the face of this, what if you were called "a resister" and told: "to get on board." How would that make you feel?

Let's be honest, **"resister" is a reductionist term.** LCD Leaders must recognize that people who resist may be doing it out of their fair analysis of an issue, their unheard ideas for improvement, their genuine care and their unmet desire to participate in decision-making.

In fact, rethinking "resisters" may prove to be your opportunity to untap a gold mine of overlooked internal resources. A multi-year study on creativity and innovation resulted in the book: "The Innovator's DNA" in which researchers outlined the five key discovery skills that characterize the most innovative entrepreneurs - (1) questioning, (2) observing, (3) experimenting, (4) networking and (5) associating. Sound familiar? Yup, often times your "resisters" are simply neglected innovators who are questioning the way we do things. This is consistent with how the book describes innovators, as individuals who:

> "...constantly ask questions that challenge common wisdom...'they get a kick out of screwing up the status quo...they can't bear it. So they spend a tremendous amount of time thinking about how to change the world. And as they brainstorm, they like to ask: 'If we did this, what would happen?'" (Dyer, 2009)

So what happens when we don't entertain these POSITIVE skills? Both to those individuals personally and to unexplored opportunities to improve our schools?

ASSEMBLE A DESIGN TEAM

DOES TEAM SIZE MATTER?

CAN YOUR TEAM PASS THE PIZZA TEST?

In 1970, Harvard Professor J. Richard Hackman and his colleague Neil Vidmar from Duke designed a study to determine the perfect team size. After having teams of a variety of sizes work together on a set of tasks, they asked the teams to self-assess whether their team was too small or too large for the tasks. After compiling the data, they came up with an optimum number. You guessed it, indeed it was precisely 4.6. But before you run down the hallways of your school searching furiously for the person who could represent the .6 portion of this ideal team, please note one thing: although this study has been quoted in hundreds of scholarly articles, when it comes to team size nearly every author follows this 4.6 number with an eloquently written set of paragraphs that can be summarized in only two words. **"It depends."**

Despite inherent variation in head count, there are some general minimums and maximums to keep in mind. On the small size, you need at least two people (I won't explain...) And, on the large size, team size shouldn't exceed a number that can't pass the well-known and widely used **"pizza rule"** in teaming from Jeff Bezos, founder and CEO of Amazon.com.

> "If you can't feed your team with two pizzas, it's too big."
>
> JEFF BEZOS,
> Amazon Founder & CEO

2   3   4   5   6   7   8   9

More important than a specific number for an "ideal" team size is the opportunity to consider how to put the right people together for a powerful LCD process.

When forming the team, ask:
"WHO MIGHT HELP US...

...consider different and unexpected perspectives regarding the targeted LX?

...develop a deep understanding of the Learners impacted by the targeted LX and help us to better empathize?"

...with the skills needed during an LCD process? Or who might have access to unexpected experts and community members who have these skills? What are those skills exactly?

...imagine, design and test solutions we may never have thought of?

DOES TEAM SIZE MATTER?

DON'T GO DARK

Given the answers to these questions, we need to develop a range for our Team size that works for our learning situation in our school community. Whether our Design Team has four members, or six or eight, it's important to keep in mind that the Design Team is a conduit to a much larger group.

Traditionally when we assemble teams in our schools to take on a special project, we call special meetings over the lunch break or work together behind closed doors at a series of after school meetings. **Our school community might be vaguely aware that _"The A-Team"_ is working away on something in the background,** but the only indicators tend to be a few vacant chairs at the table at lunch in the faculty lounge.

In his book: "The Learning Leader: How to Focus School Improvement for Better Results," Reeves contends that the most important thing school leaders need to know is how to create a team with complementary strengths. A diverse team makes decision making less risky and distributes the leadership among different talents and strengths.

> "Distributed leadership is based on trust, as well as the certain knowledge that no single leader possesses the knowledge, skills, and talent to lead an organization..."
>
> Reeves, The Learning Leader (2006, p. 28)

Learner-Centered Design is different! In LCD, each member of our Design Team is not a member of a clandestine special task force, they are both a team member **and** a gateway to a larger group of people who help us tap into a larger set of skills.

CONNECT YOUR TEAM

YOU WILL HAVE NAILED THIS STEP IF...

HOW TO NOT CRASH AND BURN ON COLLABORATION

You, as a leader have accepted your call-to-adventure. And you've assembled your crackerjack team *on paper*. It's time for the first meeting and you know that the last thing busy educators need is one more thing on their plate. You're about to hand them *their* call-to-adventure.

YOUR TASK: Lead such a powerful initial meeting that your team feels compelled to accept their call-to-adventure and head out all together on this hero's journey.

YOU WILL HAVE NAILED THIS STEP IF....

WHAT YOU SHOULD BE ABLE TO SAY	WHY YOU SHOULD BE ABLE TO SAY IT
"I don't have to leap tall buildings in a single bound or be faster than a speeding bullet." (Or as fast as SnapChat, if that didn't conjure up visions of Superman...)	You don't have to be the "be-all-end-all" for the group. You are *self*-aware - you know your strengths and weaknesses. That's why you have a team. They can backfill your gaps.
"It was like I was at a Red Sox game, getting goose bumps while singing "Sweet Caroline" with the entire crowd at Fenway Park.	Your team might not have begun this way, but they should now feel as though they connected to something that is larger than themselves - a problem worth solving.
"We all walked into the first meeting wondering why we were there, but we all walked out wondering why we hadn't tackled this problem together sooner...	We walked into the first meeting puzzled by who was in the room and left crystal clear on why each team member is a vital piece of the puzzle.
"It was so weird - everyone spoke and everyone listened! I've never seen anything like it!"	When we use *protocols* to ensure everyone has a voice, and everyone is heard, well... team members have a voice and team members are listened to. It's that easy silly.
"They love me, they really love me..." Says a team member in the hallway on their cell with their spouse, as they leave the meeting."No, no, honey, we didn't get matching tattoos........yet."	Yea, the principal asked me to be on this team but it's not like a membership to an exclusive club. It's more like belonging to an inclusive club, because the job of our team is to understand those who we are going to serve.

IS TIME FOR COLLABORATION ENOUGH?

CHAMPAGNE-WORTHY COLLABORATION

How?

"Finally, we've got collaborative time in our timetable!" Time to celebrate! Once we've found the time for educators to work together, it's the fast train to student success travelling full speed ahead, right?

Well, let's not pop that bottle of bubbly just yet.

Some words to the wise from Michael Fullan	"Collaborative cultures, which by definition have close relationships, are indeed powerful, but unless they are focusing on the right things they may end up being powerfully wrong." –Michael Fullan

How many of us have worked hard to create a collaborative model, only to have those who we have asked to work together tell us that they are frustrated with the people in their group, that preparing for another meeting is more work, that the tasks they do are meaningless and that collaborative time is something that they dread!

In "Teachers Know Best - Teachers Views on Professional Development" by the Bill and Melinda Gates Foundation, focus groups of educators were asked about their current collaborative experiences and they responded by saying things like:

"Need an agenda and rules... Otherwise it's a social hour."

"Feels like I'm being held hostage."

"People might have good knowledge but the pieces don't fit together."

"Not another meeting."

"I would rather be somewhere else."

"Not one more thing I have to do."

What were the conditions when you experienced the following?

Powerful Collaboration	Powerfully Bad Collaboration
• Time to Talk about issue in depth/breadth • Goals	Talk devolves into nothing No Goals

Sounds like we need to put together the pieces of the collaboration puzzle...

CONNECT YOUR TEAM

COLLABORATION BASICS

STOP. (NO, IT'S NOT "HAMMER TIME," SILLY...)

SELF: The Greek aphorism: *"know thyself"* sums up this piece of the puzzle. To collaborate well, we must first understand ourselves - personalities, tendencies with tasks and working with others, strengths, challenges, preferences around learning, completing tasks and more.

TASK: Imagine a team of individuals who have strong knowledge of themselves and legitimate care for one another. We might feel a sense of assurance that great collaboration is inevitable. However, the team will still fail to reach deep levels of collaboration if we fail to frame challenges, projects and tasks that are "Collaboration-Worthy" - meaning difficult enough to require collaboration, open-ended and perceived as relevant to the team.

The Collaboration Puzzle

Self

Task

Others

Protocols

OTHERS: The goal here would be to get team members to the point that they would say the following about their fellow team mates: "I know who they are as a person, I like them, I trust them and ultimately I care about their well being." How might you engage your Design Team members in activities that build care for one another? No, not trust falls and the like. Why would this piece even be necessary? Flash forward one week or one month to the inevitable team conflict - disagreements, conflicting ideas, etc. While protocols are amazing tools, it's hard to imagine that a given problem solving approach or a conflict resolution protocol would achieve much more than a shallow, superficial solution without clear personal investment in our fellow Design Team members. Hence the importance of building genuine understanding and care for others.

PROTOCOLS: Take a minute to think about the collaboration-meccas - Google, Ideo and more. They've all studied how to do collaboration well. One key causal factor for high-quality collaboration that comes up is "equity of voice." But, how do you achieve this? Norms and protocols are a good place to start! Pro Tip: Protocols can guide any of the following interactions: discussion, ideation, reflection, decision making, conflict resolution, giving and receiving feedback, tuning work and more. And guess, what?! There are tons of easy, fun and effective protocols in this book! And they can quickly be learned, taught, modelled and practiced! Too easy...

COLLABORATION BASICS

WHAT HAPPENS WHEN YOU DON'T HAVE ALL THE PIECES OF PUZZLE?

Care for **OTHERS**

ONLY "OTHERS"

If it's **only others** - relationships, knowledge of others and care for others - **then we are a coffee club**.

ONLY "TASKS"

If it's **only tasks -** products, presentations, services, solutions and more - **then we are robots**.

Worthy **TASKS**

PROTOCOLS for interactions

ONLY "PROTOCOLS"

If it's **only protocols -** norms, rituals, procedures, routines, agreements - then we are an algorithm.

ONLY "SELF"

If it's **only self -** lone wolf, rogue cowboy, solo-flyer - then we are Will Ferrell streaking through the quad...

Knowledge of **SELF**

So why collaborate? Do you believe you can build better ideas with the help of others than you could on our own? I do. But, let's get real, this "nirvana-state" of collaboration doesn't always actually happen. Harnessing the collaborative capacity of individuals in teams can be a challenge if we don't have ALL the pieces of the collaboration puzzle.

CONNECT YOUR TEAM

ADDING SURPRISE AND DELIGHT TO MEETINGS

HOW TO NOT CRASH AND BURN ON COLLABORATION

"Ok folks, what we are going to do is to have everyone introduce themselves - where they are from, what they do in the organization and why they feel that this problem is important. Because there are eight of us, we are only going to give people two minutes each. Ok, let's start..."

Womp, womp. Ever had to do this before? Perhaps not just in a group of eight, but maybe twelve people, or even more? The first person starts, and the group smiles and listens intently while they go through each of the points for their self-introduction. The two minute mark comes and goes in a flash, as Team Member One is very passionate about the problem that lays before the group. After closer to three minutes, we move on to the second person. The group smiles again, but is listening a bit less intently while they are contemplating what they have just heard, as they simultaneously begin formulating their own responses in their heads. Another two or three minutes goes by. And another. By the time we get to the poor person who is last in the circle, 20+ minutes has passed. If we were to give the group a pop quiz on some of the details of the introductions (perhaps even just recalling first names), how much do you think each person would remember about their fellow team members?

With all due respect, we just aren't that interesting. Check that. And this sort of format is also just not that interesting. Why not ignite the creative juices of your team from the moment the first meeting begins? Voilà, 3 ready-to-go activities to jump-start the collaboration-engine and to keep it purring:

1 QUICK(ISH) DESIGN CHALLENGE:
Design Another Teammate's Autobiography Book Cover

Later, in the cross industry innovation section of Changing Change, you'll learn about finding the people and organizations who are the best in the world at something. Why bother doing this? Well, if we care about doing something well, why not look to the people who are considered best-in-the-world at that thing? Ok, back to our Design Challenge. Where in the world might you find the best "home" for a person and their story? Well, their autobiography might be a good place to start… Yes, yes, I know your teammates may not have actually written an autobiography. (Yet...) However, imagine for a minute that they had and that they hired *you* to design their book cover. How could you capture the essence of who they are and their story on 6 x 9 inches? Time to get to know who you're working with and then share it with the rest of the team!

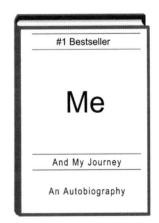

2 QUICK(*ISH*) DESIGN CHALLENGE:
Tech Blast

Want to connect a team that likes to have fun with technology? Why not have them play around with a collaborative slide deck? Grab a slide deck template *(check out www.slides-carnival.com - it's cool and free!)* and create a title slide with your project name and second slide that describes why the team has gathered. Then, create the same number of additional slides as the number of members on your Design Team. Put their names at the top of each slide. Then, place a couple of prompts on each slide like: "I am passionate about..." or "My secret talent you might not know of is..." or "The picture that best represents me is..." Let your team go wild and have fun with it! They can insert pictures, music or whatever you guide them to do. When they are done, have team members pair up and look at each other's slides so they can introduce their partner to the rest of the group. By doing this activity, not only will you connect your group, but you can use the slide deck they have created to introduce your Design Team to others so they know who is working on the project! Presto magic!

3 ONGOING APPRECIATION
Popcorn Token

During your meetings, you'll be working hard... Why not launch your second meeting with a ritual like this one. For this ritual, you must find some sort of "token." A special item that is small, portable and maybe even a bit zany. (E.g. Bobble head doll, *you're welcome for the idea...*) The idea is that this token bounces around from person to person unpredictably, like popcorn, in each meeting. "How?" You ask... Well, the person who first launches the ritual takes 3 minutes or less to publicly acknowledge another team member for a job-well-done. Perhaps they noticed this team member taking a risk or keeping an open mind or courteously opening the door for others at the end of the last meeting. For whatever reason, it stuck out in their mind. They noticed it. So, they acknowledge it, they pass the token and at the next meeting the team member now holding the token acknowledges a different team member for something admirable they had noticed. And voilà, the token "popcorns around" unpredictably, but with surprise, delight and a sprinkle of appreciation.

Pssst...
Want to try some of these or have your own ideas? Jot them down here...

SURPRISE & DELIGHT FACTOR...

HOW TO FACILITATE AWESOME MEETINGS

How many "poke-your-eyes-out-with-a-pencil-meetings" have you been to? **Exactly.** Not all meetings are created equal. Great meetings can harness collaboration and insights during an LCD process. Conversely, meetings can be overused, under-productive and a downright waste-of-time. No thanks. Use the following steps to plan for meetings that have surprise and delight and that are also productive and time-efficient.

Select Meeting Leader(s)

Who will lead and guide the meeting? Will different leaders guide different parts of the same meeting? Do you want to rotate leaders for different meetings?

Set Reasonable Time Frames

Rarely should meetings last longer than 60 minutes. Can your objectives be completed in that period of time? Are you prepared to task delegate and re-meet? Once you determine a reasonable time frame, create a schedule, share it in advance and stick to the schedule.

Create Meeting Norms & Use Protocols

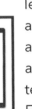

To get as much done as possible, meeting leaders should be prepared to use norms and protocols to ensure active, even and inclusive participation. Norms can also include agreements made around technology usage during a meeting. E.g. Cell phones, laptops, etc. One of our favorite norms from High Tech High School is: "tough on content, easy on people."

Determine Objectives

What do you hope to accomplish by the end of the meeting? Is a meeting really even necessary to achieve these goals?

Invite Relevant Attendees

Think carefully about who needs to attend a meeting both to (1) actively participate and also possibly for (2) transparency and input. No one wants to feel excluded from important work, and conversely no one wants to feel compelled to attend a meeting at which their presence is unnecessary.

LFM alwyss

Blow Up Boring!

Mix things up! Launch meetings with activities that model the elements of surprise and delight you'd want to see all Learners (like students) experiencing.

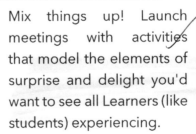

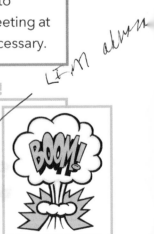

End with Appreciation & Next Steps

Meetings can be intensely productive and highly collaborative. Ensure people feel their contributions were valued and appreciated! Meetings often end with additional tasks to be completed beyond the meeting. Can everyone articulate their next steps and any deadlines?

HOW TO MAKE TOUGH DECISIONS

FOUR APPROACHES TO DECISION MAKING...

Reaching agreement doesn't always happen organically, on it's own. Sometimes reaching agreement on a approach to decision making, as a team, before starting work can increase productivity and speed of work and prevent conflict down the road.

1

CONSENSUS

Consensus is general or universal agreement. This means everyone participating in the decision making process has agreed on the same decision to be made. While consensus is often desired, it can be difficult to achieve. Consensus can be important when large decisions are being made in small groups. It can be very difficult, though not impossible, to reach in medium groups. Without time and extensive use of protocols, consensus may be unrealistic to use in large-group decision making.

2

DEMOCRATIC VOTING ✓

Multiple (more than 2) options to be voted on. More than 4 people voting. One vote per person. May the best option win.

POLLS & SURVEYS ✓ **3**

Polls and surveys can be useful when outside input is desired for decision making. If needed, polls and surveys can solicit the input of a focus group or representative sample. A poll may lead to the best decision, despite

the fact that the outcome of the polled audience may differ from the preferences of the team.

This can be useful in engineering and design of consumer goods wherein the inherent preferences of the engineers or designers are less relevant to the decisions to be made about the project.

Ranking Option

✓ **4** BORDA METHOD OF VOTING

The Borda method is useful when voting is desired, but the group is too small for a clear "winner" to emerge.

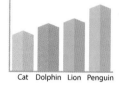

Many use Borda when there are fewer than five options on which to be voted and there are less than 8 people voting. Borda uses a ranking system, examples shown below.

Person 1

Penguin	4
Lion	3
Cat	1
Dolphin	2

Person 2

Penguin	2
Lion	4
Cat	1
Dolphin	3

Person 3

Penguin	3
Lion	1
Cat	4
Dolphin	2

Rank your choices in order, the highest indicating your top choice. Each voting member casts their "ranked votes." The option with the highest total tally becomes the "winning choice."

				Total Votes
Penguin	4	2	3	9
Lion	3	4	1	8
Cat	1	1	4	6
Dolphin	2	3	2	7

YOU WILL HAVE NAILED THIS PHASE IF...

UH OH, DOCTOR. IT LOOKS LIKE ANOTHER BAD CASE OF "SOLUTION-ITIS."

LEARNER CENTERED DESIGN
APPRECIATE · ILLUSTRATE · IDEATE · ITERATE · PROLIFERATE

Educators are busy. With all of the different challenges that come with running a school, we know that the moment we solve one problem is the moment that the next one comes running through our doors. We get it. However when we feel like we are constantly in this state of "educational triage" as school leaders, we can unintentionally develop one of the most common ailments in education, colloquially known as "SOLUTION-itis." This is the affliction that occurs when hard-working, well-meaning educators move rapidly from problem to solution, typically without involving those who will live with the solution. So how do we avoid this rampant disease? How do we avoid putting another "band-aid on a gusher?" You may find the cure in the Appreciate Phase where we learn to think "who" before "do."

YOUR TASK: To get down low to get the low-down! Look for places, find people and go into spaces so that you and your team can get the best I.N.T.E.L. you possibly can. You must create the opportunities you need in order to nail this phase!

YOU WILL HAVE NAILED THIS PHASE IF....

WHAT YOU SHOULD BE ABLE TO SAY	WHY YOU SHOULD BE ABLE TO SAY IT
"My feet are sore after walking miles in other people's shoes.... Can I have a foot rub?"	You know that to develop a deep understanding of the problem, as experienced by others, that you had to experience it alongside others.
You've been in the trenches and might have traces of nonpermanent marker on your collar or blouse.	You have realized that those who are having the problem are not just lazy complainers.
When someone asks if you've done your "ethnography," you don't reach for your phone to flash up your Instagram account.	You have recognized the real key in solving the problem is not to start solving the problem, rather it is to discover the "pain points."
"Way!," in response to a colleague who says "No way!" as you describe what your team has discovered to them.	You thought "who before do..." You and your team have developed a deep understanding of the problem and those affected. Well done!

WHAT CAN WE LEARN FROM SWIFFER?

Continuum is an internationally acclaimed design firm with offices all across the globe in Boston, Los Angeles, Milan, Seoul, and Shanghai. The clients that work with Continuum and the challenges they present are always varied and complex. From finding new ways to help children to manage their insulin levels, to skin smoothing lasers, to trying to find a low cost solution in order to provide one laptop per child, Continuum designers must work within their clients' budgets, timelines, and success metrics when developing solutions. Continuum even designed the iconic Reebok Pump! As a design firm, they do their job to solve problems for their clients very well: they have won 28 International Design Excellence Awards, and dozens more accolades.

In 1994, Proctor and Gamble (P&G) was in search of a new cleaning product. Together, they felt that the method of filling up a bucket with soap and water, soaking, squeezing, and mopping floors could be improved. P&G could have chosen to make different modifications to their current selection of mops. Their designers might have hypothesized that by creating a mop with a more ergonomically correct handle to reduce strain on the average user. They might have looked at improving mechanisms to help wring out a mop more easily. They might have guessed that jazzing up the packaging and appearance would give them an edge. Instead of reinventing their own wheel, they chose to work with Continuum to see if there was a different way. And there was!

Continuum took an approach to this problem that was beautiful in its simplicity: they went into people's homes and watched them mop. Amongst their observations, they found that people spent nearly as much time cleaning their mop as they did cleaning their floor! Through observations, they developed empathy and understanding for users and their challenges. This allowed Continuum to develop a prototype that was called "Fast Clean," which evolved into Swiffer - the ubiquitous product in most of our closets. It's even found its way into the lexicon: "I just need to swiffer the floor before our company comes for dinner!" To date Swiffer nets upwards of $500 million dollar per year in sales. Quick recap: Continuum's process to help P&G create a $500 million dollar mop was primarily watching and listening to moppers. Hmmm. In a simple, almost Seinfeld-ian way, that just makes sense, doesn't it? Ask the moppers about mopping!

So, what about us in our schools? Could we use the same process? If we want to find out how things are going in our schools, why don't we just ask the people who are experiencing our schools?

As a school leader, have you ever sat down with a focus group of students and really listened to what they thought of their classes and the school? Or with a small group of teachers to understand their perceptions of professional development days? Did you feel like you had a better understanding as a result? How do you think those individuals might have felt after their Principal sat with them to genuinely listen and appreciate their perspectives? If any of this is resonating with you, then the Appreciate Phase of LCD has your name written all over it!

P.S. If you have never done this, put your coffee cup in the space allotted (top right) to save your spot, and go convene a focus group. Listen to them. Right now. We'll wait for you.

PHASE ONE - APPRECIATE

DO YOUR I.N.T.E.L.

HOW TO BECOME AN "EDUCATIONAL ETHNOGRAPHER"

I **IMMERSE** yourself in the context with groups and individuals

N **NON-JUDGEMENT** - take out your own biases and seek to understand

T **TASKS** - observe what Learners are saying or producing as a result of tasks

E **EMPATHIZE** with Learners - observe and share in their experiences

L **LISTEN**, listen and when you think it's time to talk, listen some more

When you're doing your INTEL. **Keep in mind:**

| If we are waiting to speak, we are not listening. | Observations, not opinions. | If we already know the answers, we are asking the wrong questions. | Curiosity, not conclusions. | If we already have the solution, we are part of the problem. |

Something smells a bit funny with your INTEL...do you have GAS?

Guesswork

Assumptions

Speculation

(Well, this is a bit embarrassing.)

Good thing there's a pill for GAS.... Pretty sure it's called "genuine empathy"

www.pblconsulting.org

A PILL FOR GAS

ARE YOU REALLY EMPATHIZING WITH YOUR LEARNERS?

Why bother with first-hand experiences? To move past sympathy and imaginative empathy and arrive at powerful, genuine empathy. "What's the difference?," You ask...

SYMPATHY

Feeling compassion, pity or sorrow for others as a result of their unfortunate and/or negative experiences or suffering.

 **VERSUS**

EMPATHY

Shared understandings, emotions and feelings through shared experiences. Putting yourself into the shoes of another person to really understand those shoes.

IMAGINATIVE EMPATHY

You haven't actually had an experience comparable to the person with whom you're trying to empathize. So, you simply imagine what it would feel like or be like in that situation. This *imagined experience*, is your way of vicariously sharing in a missing experience in order to build some amount of empathy.

VERSUS

GENUINE EMPATHY

You actually have been in comparable situations or you have created opportunities to experience for yourself, first-hand, a-day-in-their-shoes. Thus, you have had a *shared experience* and can genuinely empathize with people's feelings and emotions in those situations.

GET ON THE BUS...!

What this means is that if we are targeting the LX of bus riding *(constructs aside)* and the district superintendent is on the Design Team, then the superintendent should ride the bus to and from school....a few times. We aren't spectators, we're riders. Well, actually we should be spectators and riders, because we should also observe our Learners in order to gather INTEL on what they're experiencing when riding the buses.

BE A CAMERA MAN, NOT A JOURNALIST

LEARN TO SEE, NOT JUDGE

Let's do a little activity together. Take a look at the image below and in the box below list what you're noticing.

I'm noticing....

pumpkins
heavy

If these look similar to what you wrote, then you're "noticing" and observing. Great!

I'm noticing there is one orange on the left. There are three cherries on the right. The left side of the scale is lower than the right side of the scale.

If this looks closer to what you wrote, then whoa now, you're actually inferring, drawing conclusions and even judging.

I'm noticing that the orange is heavier than the cherries.

Welcome to the Ladder of Inference. During the Appreciation Phase we need to stay low on the ladder. Learn to be a cameraman, not a journalist. You're not the journalist who is investigating, putting together the pieces of the puzzle and chasing leads about your emerging journalistic hunches.

Rather, be the cameraman who is looking, seeing, paying attention, learning to point the camera in the right direction as well as who is keeping tools and equipment up-to-date so they can capture and record what is happening....all without judgement.

SUMMARIZE YOUR CONCRETE "APPRECIATE" STEPS

HOW WILL YOU DO YOUR INTEL?

PLAN TO COLLECT DATA

PLAN INTERVIEWS & FOCUS GROUPS

PLAN OBSERVATIONS

What were Learners saying and producing? E.g. "11/13 parents sat without speaking during the last activity" versus "11/13 parents were bored during the last activity" - that is "bad GAS."

PLAN FIRST-HAND EXPERIENCES

How did you immerse yourself? Describe your first-hand experience so someone could repeat it.

- FLASH FORWARD -

You're ready to move forward when you can review and reflect on your INTEL

LEARNERS ARE SAYING...

LEARNERS ARE PRODUCING...

PATTERNS WE NOTICE...

WHAT SURPRISES US...

PHASE TWO - ILLUSTRATE

YOU WILL HAVE NAILED THIS PHASE IF...

CAUTION: ALMOST EVERYONE DOES THIS PHASE WRONG...

Now that you've appreciated the depth and breadth of the problem, it's time to set clear goals and targets for your still-unknown-solution. Sounds easy, but almost everyone will do this wrong. Instead of simply illustrating goals, we fall into the trap of inadvertent & premature ideation

The LCD leader must help the Design Team envision the taste and flavors they want to experience before they start picking recipes for their multi-course tasting menu. That means we need to ask questions that help our Learners granularize what we are after. What are we really trying to achieve? By deconstructing what an optimal dish might taste like in more granular terms, then we can begin to pull those elements out in order to carry them forward into the Ideate Phase.

YOUR TASK: Blank the canvas and use your ethnography (*not "how we've always done it"*) to help your team paint an unforgettable portrait of the ideal LX.

YOU WILL HAVE NAILED THIS PHASE IF....

WHAT YOU SHOULD BE ABLE TO SAY	WHY YOU SHOULD BE ABLE TO SAY IT
You feel like you've pictured your ideal date, but you're still sitting on the couch with a cucumber mask, eating Ben and Jerry's and wondering how and when you will actually meet them.	You've unshackled yourself from constraints so that you could simply name the features of an ideal. Now, you've wrapped your head around a clear set of goals, but remain foggy on how to achieve those goals...
If you told your bestie about your vision for Mr. Right, they would say, "that only happens in the movies." And yet you know they watch those movies every weekend.	Would you want your daughter to settle for a _____ (*fill in the blank*) soul mate? On the same line, would you want to send your own child to a school that settles for sub-par LX?
You can pin somebody to the wall at a dinner party to gush on about the characteristics of a future solution, but when they ask you, so what is it? You proudly declare: "We don't know, **yet**!"	You haven't subverted the entire Illustrate Phase. Trust the process. You have the elements of a solution, but you haven't started solving yet. The *Ideate Phase comes next* silly...

> "The difficulty lies not in the new ideas...but in escaping from the old ones." –John Maynard Keynes

TRY THINKING DIFFERENTLY

DO YOU ENJOY GETTING A SPEEDING TICKET?

Not just the physical act of receiving of the ticket, but the whole experience: from your initial gasp when you see the red and blue lights in the rear view mirror, to the stammering and coming up with your best excuse as to why you were in such a hurry, to that sinking feeling in your stomach when you make the grim realization that this time you will not be escaping with a stern warning. It is both maddening and humiliating all at once, especially when that brown minivan that you passed ten minutes ago in Mario Andretti-like fashion trundles past you when you are pulled over and lightly toots its horn, just to rub a little "obey the limit" salt into your open wound. Cue head shake.

For years, we have used the same few methods to stop people from speeding - signs, stern warnings, photo radar, and of course, the threat of getting a fine for being a bit of a lead foot. And yet, a 2008 study laughed in the face of these combined efforts showing in a study of a thousand random drivers that 100% of them thought that it was fine to exceed the posted limit by 5 mph and 36% felt that it was ok to drive at 20 mph over the limit. (Barry, 2008) Hmm. Another head shake.

> What if we took a different approach? What if it were FUN to obey the speed limit? And even a tiny bit of "fun" when we got caught? But, how could it possibly be fun to obey the speed limit?

We often lock ourselves into the same ol' ways of solving problems - taking what we currently do and trying to do it just a little bit better. Aka: Incremental improvement. Or, we do what we have always done, but just a little bit differently - a squeeze of lime on a boring beverage. What if we looked into completely different sectors to see if there were practices that we could borrow, remix and apply to our own situation? What if we decided that we weren't going to look for a wedge of lime - like bigger speed signs or more stringent ticket fines - but rather that we would adopt a completely different approach adapted from unexpected sources?

In Copenhagen, there was a particular section of road that was known to be a place where people ignored the posted speed signs. As a part of the The Fun Theory project by Volkswagen, Kevin Richardson decided to take a different approach to helping people obey the speed limit: He used a speed camera to photograph and measure the speed of all of the drivers on this stretch of road. Now using a camera to photograph drivers was not revolutionary of course, nor was the fact that the drivers who were caught speeding were levied a fine for their traffic violation. What was truly unique was that the fines collected from the speeders were put into a pot, and those who were not speeding were out into a draw for 30% of the money that was collected from speeding ticket fines! **"The Speed Camera Lottery"** was born. Drivers slowed down an average of 22% while having a totally unique enforcement experience.

If we can change the experience of getting a speeding ticket, then can we change the experience of reviewing a policy with our staff? Of parent-teacher interviews? We can. We just have to free ourselves of the constructs that tend to confine our thinking - to free ourselves of the most convenient and seductive of all "off-ramps," which often wears a disguise called: **"This is how we have always done it."**

What if we started with "the Naive Question?"

THE NAIVE QUESTION

IT'S TIME TO CLEANSE OUR PALATE...

How can we make staff meetings better? Try asking this question amongst your peers and see what kind of responses you get. I can predict a few: "Shorter!" "Cancel them altogether!" "Have beer and pretzels..." But, questions like these are limiters: whether it's a staff meeting, professional development days for our teachers, parent-teacher interviews for our parents, or assemblies for our students, when we begin by asking questions that anchor us in the current experience, we can often limit ourselves to generating solutions that corner us in the construct of the problem. **Not so fast hot shots..**

Get started instead by asking yourselves the "Naive Question:"

> If we hadn't already been doing it this way, how would we start?

In other words, if the way we are currently doing it didn't even exist, and we were going to design it, and build it, from scratch, what would we design? What would we build? What would be **the best way** to do it? Even these questions lead us into the premature-ideation-trap. So, stay with me...

For Example: Staff Meetings. Let's say you've selected "lame staff meetings," as your targeted problem. Too often, we begin this Phase with a well-intentioned, but hasty question like: "So, how can we make our staff meetings more effective?" This question, however, means we haven't challenged the construct of a staff meeting at all.

Instead of starting from the point of a staff meeting, begin by granularizing the staff meeting's *(substitute your problem here)* functions and opportunities. Then, simply describe and elaborate on the elements of worthy function and the elements of opportunities worth striving toward.

So, first things first.. It's time to kill off your constructs. Before you try to improve "lame staff meetings," ask yourself: "What are we really after?" "What are our goals?" "What are we trying to achieve?" Staff meetings may not be the best format to achieve those goals. To be able to pursue the questions above, you must first disentangle yourselves from your preconceived constructs. They don't have to die forever...if they are worthy of being a part of your solution, you can revive them from the dead later...

YOUR CONSTRUCT GRAVEYARD (R.I.P.)

IF YOU CAN'T OBSERVE IT, IT'S NOT THERE..

WE WILL KNOW OUR SOLUTION IS SUCCESSFUL WHEN WE OBSERVE:

It's been a difficult day for everyone. The tears have happened. People have said their goodbyes. And after much suffering, as a group we slowly shuffle away from the graveyard. The constructs have been killed off and it's time for us to think about what life could be like if we didn't think of "lame staff meetings" anymore. The clouds begin to part, and the steam rises from the ground as the sun breaks through the heavens and turns the construct graveyard into a beautiful field of.....ok, ok, time to kill off this analogy, as well. Got it.

Once we have "killed our constructs" what the heck are we supposed to do now? We've always thought of staff meetings as, well... staff meetings! Let's look a bit more closely at the example of staff meetings - why do we have them? What is their function? If we were to list a few of these functions, we might come up with something like this:

To get a sense of what is happening	To learn and to share	To communicate and to discuss issues	To solve problems	To develop connections and to recognize people or groups

Let's assume that we don't just want to do these things, we want to do these things *well*. In fact, we want people to be "surprised and delighted" so that the LX is consistently sky-high for each of our Learners. Consider one function: "To learn and share." If we close our eyes for a moment and imagine a time when we observed a group of people *(any group - not necessarily at school)* learning so effectively that we can vividly remember the experience. Think back and ask: What were they saying? What were they producing? Feel free to jot some things down:

Bottom line: Getting fine-grained about what we could observe Learners saying and doing during a High Impact Learning Experience helps us plan better LX. In other words: The more we can name our ideal, High-LX success criteria in terms that are observable to us, the more likely we will know the right High-LX solution when we see it! Sample High-LX Success Criteria stems:

Our educators will be... (saying/ doing)	Our students will be... (saying/ doing)	Our parents will be... (saying/ doing)	Our community will be... (saying/ doing)	Our survey data or attendance statistics will show

CREATE YOUR LX VISION & TARGETS

GENERATE YOUR SUCCESS CRITERIA WITH "MAD LIBS"

Step One	Step Two	Step Three
Who is touched by this? Who is this LX for?	How might they be feeling during the current LX?	WILD CARD (optional)

SUCCESS CRITERIA ELEMENTS

Step One Example:
- Young children
- Teenagers
- Millennials
- (Adults)
- New parents
- Visitors
- Leaders
- Trustees
- (Teachers)

Step Two Example:
- (Nervous)
- Excited
- (Anxious)
- Serious
- Entertained
- Tired
- Disenfranchised
- Ambivalent
- (Curious)
- Angry
- Delighted

EXAMPLE

How can we design a High Impact LX for

Teachers (who are adults)

who are currently feeling

nervous, anxious & also a bit curious...

while keeping in mind

_____

PUT IT ALL TOGETHER...PART ONE: How can we design a High Impact LX for teachers who are currently feeling nervous, anxious & a bit curious...

YOUR TURN

How can we design a High Impact LX for

_____
_____

who are currently feeling

_____
_____

while keeping in mind

_____
_____

USE THIS TOOL TO GENERATE YOUR SUCCESS CRITERIA. AND PRESTO MAGIC, YOU WILL HAVE YOUR VISION OF SUCCESS AND CAN MOVE TO THE IDEATION PHASE.

Step Four

What would Learners would be saying and producing during and as a result of the LX?

Saying Example:

"Personalization looks like _____"

"I now feel confident about_____"

"I used to think _____, but now I think _____"

"I want to practice _____"

"We need to get started on this right away."

Producing Example:

Project

Suggestions / Input

Performance / Service / Demos

Drafts / Solutions

Step Five

WILD CARD *(optional)*
What additional attributes would describe the results of the LX?

Example:

...because...

...during...

...after...

...to align with...

...inspired from...

...in a way that is...

...

Step Six

How much time do we have?

Example:

One minute

Five minutes

One hour

Two hours

Half-day PD

Full day PD

One meeting

A series of meetings

1-Year Process

3-Year Strategic Plan

5-Year Time Span

---

after which Learners
will say / produce

"I want to try the new strategies we just practiced & designed!"

"...because I think it'll increase engagement."

as a result of this
experience that lasts

one full day.

PART TWO: ...after which they will say: "I want to practice the new strategies we just practiced & designed, because I think it'll increase engagement" as a result of this experience that lasts one full day?

---

after which Learners
will say / produce

as a result of this
experience that lasts

_____

_____

PHASE THREE - IDEATE

YOU WILL HAVE NAILED THIS PHASE IF...

IDEATION, FINALLY THE MOMENT YOU'VE BEEN WAITING FOR!

Now that you've appreciated the depth and breadth of the problem, killed off some constructs and established success criteria for your still-murky-solution, you now have the green light to ideate! This Phase can be fun. So, grab a coffee, hang around for a bit, try lots of new techniques and trust the process!

YOUR TASK: Create the conditions and lead activities to generate the maximum number of ideas. Every moment that an idea has to wait to be surfaced is a moment (and potentially an idea) lost.

YOU WILL HAVE NAILED THIS PHASE IF....

WHAT YOU SHOULD BE ABLE TO SAY	WHY YOU SHOULD BE ABLE TO SAY IT
You've generated DOZENS of ideas.	The first ideas are usually NOT the best ideas.
Based on others' feedback your P:E Ratio is high. (P:E is the Puke-to-Excitement Ratio.)	Why bother pursuing an idea that your team, and others, aren't slightly fanatical about...
At least one of these ideas makes you say "whoa, that's different..."	Congratulations! You've all pushed yourselves out of your comfort zone.
You keep raving about surprising ways non-educators in other industries are creatively achieving goals, like yours from Phase 2.	You've bursted the "teacher-happy place" bubble we often live in and explored possibilities in unexpected places.
Due to schools of ideas swimming around your mind, you now have a journal on your night stand to jot things down as a necessary sleep-loss prevention technique.	You stuck with Phase 3 long enough to actually live and breath it. Your current probability of having landed on some great ideas is now officially high.
You can explain why the 2-5 ideas you're carrying forward to the Iterate Phase are the most viable.	Viable relates back to the targets you set in the Illustrate Phase. Have you even checked those...?

 "I can't understand why people are frightened of new ideas. I'm frightened of the old ones." –John Cage

QUESTIONS TO IGNITE CREATIVE JUICES

IDEATION MIGHT START WITH CURIOUS QUESTIONS...

Now that you've appreciated the depth and breadth of the problem, killed off some constructs and set clear goals and targets for your still-murky-solution, you now have the green light to ideate. This Phase can be fun. So, grab a coffee, hang around for a bit, try lots of techniques and trust the process!

Some questions to get the juices flowing...

That means NON-educator...
think other industries...

If we hadn't already been doing it this way, how would we start?

Who's the best in the world at achieving our goals?

Are there really cool things *(that may not seem related to our goals)* **that could be remixed into an idea?**

What might be some unusual ways to do it?

Where might we find examples of people working together on meaningful tasks that make a genuine impact, both inside and outside of the school system? What are their measures of success? How do they go from idea to reality? What can we learn to bring back to our school?

Where might we look for inspiration and possibilities?

Where might we find examples of high performing teams, both inside and outside of education? How do they do it so well? What can we learn?

Pssst...
Yup, this is your cue again.
Write down all of your
ideas as fast as you can.
No judging ideas yet...

EARLY IDEAS & LEADS...

IDEATION MEANS THINKING DIFFERENTLY

GREAT IDEAS USUALLY DON'T EMERGE UNTIL THE THIRD WAVE.

Tina Seelig, who taught creativity and entrepreneurship at Stanford's dSchool for years, facilitated an activity in a presentation recently. She asked about 40 attendees in the first few rows of the theater packed with over 100 attendees to stand up. She gave them a task:"I'm going to give you three minutes to organize yourselves by birth date. From January 1st over here to December 31st over there." (I know...yawn, we've seen this before...) But then, **she threw in a twist**.

> She said, "But, here's the thing, **you can't talk.** Ok, time's started, GO!"

40 people stood there for a few seconds, dumbstruck, and then it happened: One person came up with an idea - they held up their fingers to indicate the number of their *month of birth*. E.g. 3 fingers equals March. Within seconds, the idea spread like wildfire. Then, it evolved, once the all the 6s congregated (representing June) they naturally transitioned to using their fingers to indicate their *day of birth* so that someone born on the 10th could get in line in relationship to someone born on the 27th. I'm sure you're starting to infer where this idea would work easily and where it might get trickier, given the 10-digit average...

By the end of the 3 minutes, the 40 people had made some progress. But, after a quick check, Tina found their overall results were inconsistent. Then, she challenged them. She said their approach was predictable. She's seen before, multiple times. It's a metaphor for most ideation: **We almost always go with our FIRST ideas. But, our first ideas are not usually the BEST ideas.** She asked the 100+ spectators in the theatre, if not with finger-signing, how else could you have overcome the constraint of "no talking?" What other work-arounds could you have thought of?

Pausing the story here for a quick minute of "reader think-time."

> What work-arounds can you think of? (Without looking at the answers at the bottom of the page.... this isn't 9th Grade Algebra, silly)

You may have noticed that you came up with a few ideas and then ideation dwindled out. Normal. And yet, how did that make you feel? Did you doubt your creative capacity?

Well, the same thing happened with 100+ spectators. They came up with a good number of ideas and then the ideation petered out. This is predictable. I'd like to introduce you to the first wave of ideas. Tina expertly coaxed out a second wave and then after a lot of awkward silence, a third wave. Importantly, it is *sometimes* in the second wave and *more often* in the third wave that the BEST ideas emerge. In order to get beyond the obvious and into a third wave, we actually have to start unravelling underlying constructs embedded into the way we are thinking about a task and its constraints.

WHY DOES RICH IDEATION OCCUR SO RARELY? Perhaps we don't know any better because we haven't had opportunities to practice ideation-done-well, nor seen it modelled. We tend to dislike awkward silence. When we are asked to generate ideas and draw a blank, we judge ourselves. It can feel uncomfortable to "not know..." (yet, at least.) And more...

Let's imagine you generate 72 ideas during YOUR Ideate Phase. What percentage of those ideas do you think will be outstanding? Ten percent? Six? Two? Exactly, if you go with your FIRST idea - number 1/1 - what's the statistical probability that it's an outstanding idea? What's the likelihood that you've unravelled thinking and broken down constraints?

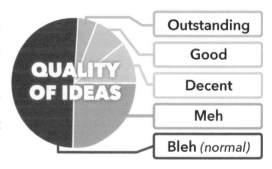

MORAL OF THE STORY: Don't automatically go with your FIRST idea(s.) This is a numbers game. **Don't sidestep the processes of ideation.** There are dozens of amazing processes in this section for you to try. Yes, these processes may be new to you, but give 'em a try. They are fun and effective. Use them to generate dozens of ideas. Then, weigh the merits of all the ideas at the end based on your success criteria from the Illustrate Phase to distil down to the BEST ideas!

SECOND MORAL OF THE STORY: Did you already launch into those curious questions on the previous page? Did you experience the first wave of ideas? Did you persevere through some long, awkward silence? Did you make it to a second wave? A third? It's ok if you didn't, few people who haven't been specifically taught to do this and then been given multiple practice opportunities would achieve a second or third wave. After all, stopping after a first wave seems natural. But, now that you know...maybe it's time to return to those questions for another go at it... Or should I say at least **two** more rounds. Time to get comfortable with awkward silence.

PHASE THREE - IDEATE

BRAINSTORMING WHEN YOU HAVE NO IDEAS (YET)

100 IDEAS IN 10 MINUTES

Use this approach when there are a lot of participants and you're still early in the process. This works best when there are still tons of directions and possibilities for solutions.

Pssst...
Want to try some of these? But, maybe feeling out of your comfort zone? That's ok, just start by starting.

TRY IT

Name a few scribes who can take down 10-20 ideas each on separate sheets of chart paper or sections of a white board. Set a timer for ten minutes. The group calls out ideas and the scribes call back the idea they are going to write down to avoid duplicates. Ten minutes later, you can have 100+ ideas.

PICK ONE...OR TWO...

WORD LISTING

Get out your trusty thesaurus

Free association of words related to and contrary to your idea can help generate new and useful ideas and extensions to your ideas.

THREE METHODS TO GET STARTED

STEP 1

Create three columns on a white board, a piece of chart paper or even just a simple sheet of paper. In the first column, write the prompt, question, problem or key area of focus for your project or challenge. Then write words, ideas and concepts that are related to your prompt.

STEP 2

Review what you wrote in the first column and select the word, idea or concept that resonates with you the most. Place what resonated with you at the top of the second column and then think of words, ideas and concepts related to that, and list them in the second column.

STEP 3

The third column is "opposites world" in which you'll list words, concepts and ideas that are the opposite of what you wrote in the first column. Think about antonyms, opposites and contradictions. Sometimes this gets zany, which can be fun!

STEP 4

Look for and visually connect patterns and relationships between all three columns. You're looking for that "ah ha" moment now!

4 PHASES

Use the 4 phases in order, beginning with (1) fluency, then (2) flexibility, then (3) originality & finally end with (4) elaboration on the best ideas.

Time constraints can actually increase the flow of ideas. As in 2-5 minutes per phase.

1 - 2 - 3 - 4

BRAINSTORMING FOR TODDLER-IDEAS

YES, AND . . . .

Also known as "plussing" This is based on the golden rule of improv...where you must accept what someone offers you and build off of it.

STEP 1

Form a circle with a group of about 4-16 participants. Then, name the prompt, challenge or problem to be addressed. Allow for what may feel like a period of awkward silence until the first person in the group names a possible solution or idea.

STEP 2

Now, proceed clockwise around the circle to build on the first idea by saying, "yes, and..." Essentially, you are "plussing" the idea. Continue to develop the idea in this manner until the ideation momentum dies out. Go with what you have or do another round until you feel you can move forward in the project process.

FOUR METHODS TO DEVELOP EARLY IDEAS

FUTURE THINKING

Future thinking is all about challenging the conventions in our present world. Start this type of brainstorming with a semi-developed idea/design in mind. Then, flash forward one year, two years, ten years to imagine how the idea/design could be improved in the absence of the constraints of our present day lives and world.

MAD LIBS

This brainstorming technique is based on the game Mad Libs.

Create a quick Mad Lib frame that is relevant to your semi-developed idea/design. Include lots of blanks.

ROLE PLAYING

Role playing as an approach to brainstorming is exactly what it sounds like. Get two or more people together to act out how a semi-developed idea/design would be discussed, used and/or experienced by a potential user.

TRY IT

E.g. The _____ reminds me of _____ and _____ because _____.

Do the same frame multiple times, or let other people give it a try after hearing about your idea/design.

Try to tease out some patterns. This can be a fun prompt to use in a focus group.

TRY IT

During the role play, think about the behaviors, feelings, questions, pain points and more that participants are experiencing. Does this give you ideas for how you could revise your idea/design? This approach is particularly useful when you are developing services.

PHASE THREE - IDEATE

BRAINSTORMING METHODS WHEN YOU'RE STUCK

STEP 1

Generate an umbrella term that captures the essence of your overall challenge or project.

STEP 2

Now, jot down the first thing - one word, idea, concept, adjective or item - that comes to mind when you think about that umbrella term.

STEP 3

Now consider the umbrella term and the new word together. Engage in free association to attempt to generate new connections, patterns or ideas

STEP 4

Rinse and repeat until, hopefully, you achieve a breakthrough!

BRUTETHINK

Ever get stuck in a creative process?

Use this technique to help get "unstuck."

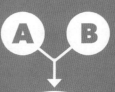

TWO METHODS FOR WHEN YOU'RE STUCK

Pssst...
You know the drill.
Jot down your faves below.
Try tagging members of your team to lead one...

IDEA INVERSION

OPPOSITES

WORLD

Try flipping your idea on its head...

Though seemingly counter-intuitive, sometimes the best breakthroughs happen when you think of the opposites of your target.

TRY IT

Like with the word listing method, this approach requires spending some time in opposites world. Consider an idea or concept that isn't working well, or perhaps take the problem that your project or design challenge is attempting to solve. Now, think about achieving the exact opposite of the goal. Elaborate all the possible variations of the opposite by listing words, adjectives, protocols, procedures, concepts and steps that would foster the opposite. Sometimes, in doing this we identify the necessary mechanisms to achieve the opposite. If we flip that, we can sometimes breakthrough on how to achieve the actual target.

WHAT WILL YOU TRY?

BRAINSTORMING METHODS THAT GET VISUAL!

MIND MAPPING

A visual method of brainstorming that helps individuals or groups name and connect a variety of diverse ideas and concepts to find trends and patterns.

STEP 1

To begin this visual brainstorming process, write the prompt, question, problem or key focus in the center of a white board, a piece of chart paper or even just a simple sheet of paper.

STEP 2

Jot down words, concepts, ideas and more in a way that connects them to the central prompt and that connects them to one another. If you run out of ideas, try creating a section that lists words, concepts and ideas that are the opposite of your area of focus.

STEP 3

Continue to freely build out the various extensions from the original prompt by naming related words, concepts and ideas.

STEP 4

Review the range of ideas, look for trends and patterns in order to gather and build on the best ideas.

THREE VISUAL BRAINSTORMING METHODS

COMIC STRIPS

This approach to brainstorming is all about empathizing with the user experience.

By simply imagining how users would view and use a product, concept or service we can gain insight on how to advance the idea.

STEP 1

Get started by sketching a user or scene of users in a cartoon-like format with speech bubbles. Capture potential environment and activities that would be going on. Can't sketch well? You can use a printed pictures instead.

STEP 2

Now, imagine and include dialog to what is now a storyboard in a way that mirrors the potential user experience. It may look like a comic strip.

STEP 3

What can you learn from the story to improve your idea? Keep referencing this comic strip during your design project. You can change the dialog, as needed.

PICTURE ASSOCIATION

This method of visual brainstorming relies on pictures and other visual materials as a source of inspiration for generating new and useful ideas.

STEP 1

Getting started with this method requires a bit of homework. You'll need to print out a variety of pictures - they can be photos, sketches, graphics and illustrations. They should be related to your challenge or project. You can get materials for web searches, books, magazines and more.

STEP 2

Now organize all of the materials you printed into like-groupings. How are they related? Name each grouping to capture the interconnectedness. These groups can be remixed and renamed numerous times in an effort to find new patterns and categories of likeness.

STEP 3

Use the process until you feel inspired to run with an idea for your challenge.

THREE WORDS: CROSS. INDUSTRY. INNOVATION.

Yup, that's a thing. As busy leaders and educators inside of our schools and school districts, we rarely get the opportunity to see how things are done outside of the field education. Let's be honest, it's pretty difficult to hit the pause button for long enough to grab a sandwich and a bathroom break, never mind to take a peek over the fence at what other industries do that have similar challenges to us in the school system!

When we begin to move outside of the school system into areas like business and industry for inspiration, it is not uncommon for us as teachers and school leaders to have a visceral reaction: "Wait a second...schools aren't businesses! Heck, we're not making widgets here, these are real people!" we shout. Well, you're right, our schools need not be considered businesses and we certainly *do not* produce widgets. Yet, LCD leaders and their Design Teams know that in order to be truly innovative in education, there is absolutely nothing wrong with looking outside of education to different fields or industries *(which may include business)* that do certain things really well in order to get inspiration and to discover things that we can borrow. This is called "Cross-Industry Innovation," and innovators do this all of the time!

As Ramon Vullings says in his thought-provoking book "Not Invented Here: Cross Industry Innovation."

> "The best way to develop ideas is to look at other places. Spend time learning from other markets, other sectors. Apply the best ideas from one sector to another."

Think about it...if schools had to assemble something really quickly, over and over again (think report card packages, or gift bags for a community fundraiser), what could we learn something from watching a Formula One Pit Stop or a Fast Food Restaurant Drive-Thru?

Think about it...could we address the untapped capacity of our students and staff members sitting in our classrooms and staff meetings the same way that two moms looked at the untapped potential of cars that sit unused in parking lots most of the day to fuel their vision

of ZipCar? **Or perhaps we could get inspiration from the wildly successful car-sharing service that has helped thousands of people around the world?** In innovation, we must rethink problems as opportunities for our new and interesting solutions. We must learn to look in odd places to connect seemingly disparate ideas in new ways to solve old problems.

ARE YOU READY TO MOVE ON?

CROSS. INDUSTRY. INNOVATION.

Think about it... Could we address at the dead twenty-minutes prior to our elementary school winter concerts like movie theaters use the twenty minutes prior to a movie to speak to the people who have gotten there early to secure their seats? (Probably more like 45 minutes prior if we are thinking about schools - every parent wants the best seat to see their little angels!) What could we do with that time? LCD leaders and their Design Teams know they need to think differently, and that they need to look for that different thinking inside AND outside of education.

YOUR TURN! Jot down what these different entities do really well, and what schools could learn from them. Remember, we are not here to judge, we are here to LEARN!

What is it?	What do they do well?	How can we adapt or apply this?
Starbucks		
Your Fave Restaurant		
Pixar		
Your Fave Relative		
Apple		
Wild Card (you pick)		

Are we ready to move on to Iterate?

First things first, let's double check the "Nailed It" criteria. At the end of the Ideate Phase, we want to be ready to move a few of our ideas that have the best chance of meeting our Success Criteria **FROM** a concept that we can imagine in our minds, TO something that our Learners can experience. It is vital that we turn our ideas into things that are tangible. Picture yourself *telling* a friend about a great idea that you have for a cell phone holder that clips onto the armrest in his car: if you can only describe your idea, you might get feedback like "It sounds ok, but I can't really picture it. Is that even possible?" However, imagine giving your friend something that is real, so he can pick it up, hold it, put his phone in it and try it out in his car. Now he will actually be able to give you useful feedback on how well your idea works. At the conclusion of the Ideate Phase, we need to have ideas that meet our Success Criteria from the Illustrate Phase and that can be experienced by the Learner. Are your ideas ready to be experienced?

YOU WILL HAVE NAILED THIS PHASE IF...

"GET OFF OF THE WHITE BOARD AND GET INTO THE REAL WORLD." -Saul Kaplan

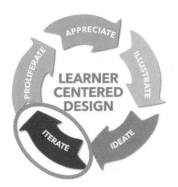

In his humorous keynote addresses to educators around the globe, international thought leader Simon Breakspear, founder of Agile Schools, often reminds us about how happy he is to be the second-born child in his family. "We all know about the first pancake," he jokes, "it never usually turns out all that well!" And while all of us second siblings around the world might laugh, his point is spot-on when it comes innovation: we need to come to grips with the fact that the first time we try something, there is a good chance it won't turn out the way we might have expected.

In the Iterate Phase of Learner-Centered Design, it is vital for us to go against what seems to be the norm in education. Ahem, that would be the **"know, then do" philosophy**. Once we have appreciated the challenge, illustrated the vision and ideated possible solutions, the only way for us to know if we have hit the mark for our Learners is to DO! That means we need to create something that people can actually try out, to "kick the tires" in real-time so we can observe and listen to feedback. And then improve!

We must adopt a "do, so I can know" approach where we are willing to try out our ideas with mindsets that are hungry for feedback. This approach lets us see how an idea works so that we can tweak it and make it better.

YOUR TASK: As Saul Kaplan would say, "Get off the whiteboard and get into the real world!" Get the prototype to the people, we won't know if it works until Learners try it!

YOU WILL HAVE NAILED THIS PHASE IF....

WHAT YOU SHOULD BE ABLE TO SAY	WHY YOU SHOULD BE ABLE TO SAY IT
You are not staring at a piece of paper, trying to make your idea perfect.	Pro Tip: Your idea wasn't perfect. Letting people test it out and tell you about it will get it closer to ideal.
You have not gotten down on one knee and placed a ring on your idea. You're still open-minded.	Treat your idea like a speed date, and you'll increase the probability of finding a suitable "Mr. Right" that actually meets "babe-licious" criteria.
You aren't hungry for feedback, you are like post-triathlon starving for feedback.	Feed-forward, not feedback. Time spent gathering intel about what works (and what doesn't!) is time saved undoing the quadruple granny-knot on the back end.

EXPERIMENTAL LEADERSHIP

DON'T BE AFRAID TO TRY OUT YOUR IDEA

This points to one of the key challenges that school leaders must overcome in education: too often, we believe that we must make something "perfect" before we use it in our schools. "Students aren't guinea pigs!" we cry. We go on: "We need to be extremely careful with what we try in our classrooms; children are a parent's most precious commodity!" We spend weeks, creating lengthy, properly spaced and meticulously cited plans, we argue over the tiniest of details. We try and predict who will resist the change and what they will say, we craft potential responses. The next thing we know, months have passed and our Cadillac-of-an-idea is still sitting in the garage, waiting to be taken for a test drive. And yet another graduating class walks across the stage at commencements, none the wiser about how we were going to change their experience of school.

We can do better.

Of course children are precious, no one is denying that! No one is suggesting that schools pump some airborne, experimental memory drug through their ventilation systems, or attempt mass hypnosis of

Grade 3 students to increase test scores (please don't do either of those). Trying different approaches to parent-teacher interviews that involve increasing the student-parent interactions, doing a project-based learning unit that involves beautifying the local neighbourhood park, or using immersive activities at staff meetings that require our educators to do something other than "sit-n-get" are "risks" that we can and need to take!

Often times, the biggest consequences for a leader doing "high stakes" activities such as these are an elevated heart rate, a red face and a slightly bruised ego.

Ronald Heifetz is the Founding Director of the Center for Public Leadership at the John F. Kennedy School of Government at Harvard University. Heifetz describes the importance of leaders seeing their work as experiments.

"When you view leadership as an experiment, you free yourself to see any change initiative as an educated guess, something that you have decided to try but that does not require you to put an immovable stake in the ground." - The Practice of Adaptive Leadership (Heifetz, 2009, p2)

In his book The Business Model Innovation Factory, innovator Saul Kaplan agrees. Saul describes several key principles about transformation that should truly resonate with us as school leaders:

It's a user-centered world, design for it	A decade is a terrible thing to waste	Tweaks won't do it	Get off the whiteboard and into the real world	Experiment all the time

When it comes to changing the experience of change and changing the LX in our schools, a decade IS a terrible thing to waste. How many more times can we say: "We DO need to get started on this, but we probably won't get it implemented in time for our eleventh or twelfth graders."

But there is something else.

SO, WILL IT WORK?

WHAT IF OUR IDEA DOESN'T HIT THE MARK?

As school leaders, we can all relate to the idea of "the immovable stake" that Heifetz refers to. It's that time when we feel as though we've really "nailed it." At the end of the Ideate Phase, you might feel this way. So, what if during the Iterate Phase, when we are prototyping, we discover that our idea isn't hitting the mark for Learners?

Cue: Record scratch, music stops.

Just think - by now in the LCD process, we will have gone through the phases of Appreciate, Illustrate, and Ideate, and we will have created possible solutions that, on paper, seem picture perfect. Not to mention that by now, we will have likely spent enormous amounts of time and resources in the development of these ideas, only to find that once implemented they may not work out the way we originally thought. Or perhaps they work, but they create unintended, unanticipated and unwanted new problems. Ugh.

Because we had already committed so much energy and effort on this "immovable stake," we may be tempted to continue with it anyway, holding our collective noses in the hopes that we might extricate ourselves from the "rabbit hole" we had erroneously gone down. Not a great place to be, and we certainly don't want to carve our initials there.

Thus, there may be a strong temptation for you to side-step a proper Iteration Phase and to simply move into the "Celebrate Phase" (which doesn't really officially exist.)

Stop.

Iteration is one of the most critical points in the LCD process, and one where most of use fall into the same trap. Celebrating our work at this point represents what we might call a "seductive off-ramp."

Imagine, we try out our idea, we do a quick debrief afterward, we share our observations on how things went, congratulate ourselves on finally finishing, check off another item on the "to do" list and move on to the next task.

This is a mistake.

SO, WILL IT WORK?

THREE WORDS: FRAME. OF. REFERENCE.

As hard as it might be to hear, if we are striving to truly serve the Learner in LCD, then our hard work and task completion are not sufficient measures of success.

This can be a very difficult (and often polarizing) piece for school leaders to hear. When we work hard at something, we want people to appreciate our efforts. Even **constructive criticism can feel like an attack** because we are personally vested in the process. I felt like my opinion was valid: I had spent a great deal of time researching the problem and coming up with what I felt was the most effective way for the school community to deal with it. Yet, as LCD Leaders, our opinion of how we felt the experience went for the group could be completely different than the actual experience that was had by the learner. Is it valid for us to say that our classes are engaging without collecting feedback from our students? Does our opinion of the user-friendliness of our website really matter all that much if the primary user of our website is the public?

In practical terms, imagine you were having a pool installed at your house while you were away on vacation, but you came home and found that the company had put it in your front yard as opposed to in the back where you had asked it to be placed: they thought it looked better out front. While they may have thought it looked better there, worked hard to install it, were happy with the final product, they missed the mark with the person that mattered the most. You.

In the Iterate Phase, LCD Leaders know the only way to know if the solution works is to test it with those who will actually use it. The immovable stake that we need to drive in the ground is not around our idea for the best solution. It needs to be anchored in a solution that is actually achieving the success criteria for Learners we developed in the Illustrate Phase.

Feeling deflated? That's not the point here. The point is we have an opportunity during the Iterate Phase to turn our best IDEAS into real SOLUTIONS. That means tuning, tweaking, refining and sometimes overhauling our ideas. Also, sometimes, our ideas don't work well, even after we iterate them. Sometimes they cause unintended consequences. All is not lost though! We can return to our other ideas from the Ideate Phase. Remember...you generated DOZENS of ideas?! Get started iterating with some easy and effective tools, like SCAMPER, in the Iterate Phase!

ITERATE YOUR IDEAS INTO REAL SOLUTIONS

Need to "tune" your idea? (Tune means improve an idea in development, like tuning a guitar..) Try using SCAMPER - a good ol' mnemonic device to help you remember all these amazing iteration tools and tricks. Let's practice using SCAMPER with "staff meetings."

Substitute something
EX: Substitute a meeting agenda for a four-course, prix-fixe dinner menu. Staff members could select what they wanted to pursue from set options.

Combine it with something
EX: Combine staff meetings with a fitness activity (like yoga or walking.) Now our staff could get a physical and a mental workout at the same time.

Adapt something to it
EX: Take an element of something our Learners *love* and remix the essence of that into staff meetings.

Modify or magnify it
EX: Modify staff meetings to include students so they could help us solve problems we face in our school together. Then, magnify the problems (fictitiously take to an extreme) to gain insight.

Put it to some other use
EX: Use periodic staff meetings to improve something in our community.

Eliminate something
EX: Ditch staff meetings altogether.

Reserve or rearrange it
EX: Set an element of staff meetings to the sidelines if you're not ready to eliminate it, but you're not yet sure how to fix it. Think: Temporary back burner.

ARE YOU READY TO MOVE ON?

DILEMMA PROTOCOL

STEP 1 - Prep-Protocol Work: Reflect on your dilemma. First things first, Is your "dilemma" actually a dilemma? Is it puzzling, conceptual and a nut you can't manage to crack with your existing arsenal of nutcrackers? Check? Ok let's get started. Jot down some thoughts about the dilemma - imagine you were trying to explain it to someone who had no background. What's the context? Who's involved? What IS working? What's not working? Do you (*partially*) know why? Have any hunches? What have you tried to solve? What worked? What didn't? What questions do you have? Now, frame a clear focusing question that captures the essence of the dilemma and throw it on a one-pager summary of your thoughts for your consultancy group.

STEP 2 - Conduct Dilemma Protocol: Provide your consultancy group (about 3-6 peeps) with your one-pager. Allow them to quietly review. (5-10 mins) Then, share your thoughts. Your group can ask clarifying questions (*just the facts, ma'am*) then, you can respond. (5 mins). Ok, now they can ask probing questions (*require reflection and don't have clear answers*) (5-10 mins). Now restate your focusing question so everyone doesn't chase irrelevant tangents. Now you get to be a fly-on-the-wall. Turn your back to your peeps and listen while they discuss your dilemma. They can discuss what they heard, questions the dilemma raises, ideas to try, what they might do in a similar situation, suggestions and more (10-20 mins).

STEP 3 - Reflect: Summarize what you heard the group share. Perhaps you can verbally categorize feedback, notice trends, follow-up on promising nuggets and thank them for trying to help you (5-10 mins). Debrief the protocol: what worked, what you'd do differently, etc. (5 mins).

Are we ready to move on to Proliferate?

First things first, let's double check the "Nailed It" criteria. Now, let's also consider the idea that once we have completed the Iterate phase, we should feel confident in our LCD solution for two reasons: First, it meets the Success Criteria that we developed in the Illustrate Phase. Second, it *observably* demonstrated success when we actually tested our idea with Learners! Furthermore, we asked our Learners to give us honest, specific and descriptive feedback on our LCD solutions because we were insatiably curious to understand how we might make it better for them. Cool (constructive) feedback was viewed positively - we would rather fail fast and pivot with our test groups at this stage rather than take a solution fraught with problems and try to implement it at scale. Warm feedback was formative too! All in all, we did make our idea better. As LCD Leaders, if our teams have satisfied our test groups and satisfied our Success Criteria, then it's time to create the Learning Experience (LX) that will proliferate our LCD solution.

YOU WILL HAVE NAILED THIS PHASE IF...

WOULD RATHER READ THE RECIPE OR EAT THE BBQ?

Franklin's BBQ in Austin, TX is *arguably* one of the most famous BBQ restaurants in the U.S. *(Not trying to start a fight here...)* Imagine you went to Austin, TX to sample their world-class BBQ yourself. It was amazing. Your foodie bucket list is now complete. You head back home wanting to share your BBQ adventures with your family back in the 'burbs. **What do you think they'd rather experience...?**

Scenario One: Listening to you give a history lesson about the restaurant, showing everyone pictures of you eating ribs (with BBQ sauce dripping down your face), bragging about your selfie from the BBQ master's surprise cameo appearance and giving everyone postcards from the gift shop.

Scenario Two: Eating BBQ that you prepared with a recipe from Franklin's cookbook and some BBQ sauce you snagged to bring home to use for this special occasion. Now, *they* have rib sauce dripping off *their* chins and want the recipe so they can show *their* friends how great the BBQ is...

If you have a solution that no one understands, "eats" *(experiences)* or appreciates, then...well, if a tree falls in the forest... An LCD leader knows that **HIGH LX** is the master key that unlocks a door. On one side of the door is the place where ideas only live *(and sometimes die)* in our heads and on the other side is the place where solutions really come to life for our Learners.

YOU WILL HAVE NAILED THIS PHASE IF....

WHAT YOU SHOULD BE ABLE TO SAY	WHY YOU SHOULD BE ABLE TO SAY IT
You used to think "I have a lot of material to cover in today's in-service," but now you think: **"How would they learn this best?"**	Think beyond the days of "coverage...." Don't you remember tenth grade algebra....?
You're not feeling as though you're some educational evangelist who has to convince the masses that your LCD solution is worthy.	A high LX proliferation of an LCD solution is like a great restaurant: no need for a big sign that says, "We make great food!" The LCD solution, like the dining experience, should speak for itself. Your "customers" will *want* to tell everyone about it.
After designing your Proliferation LX, your Design Team can't stop saying to each other before the launch: **"I can't wait to see the look on their faces!"**	If you wouldn't be excited to do the LX you designed, do you think staff will be? And after a long day of teaching? Seriously…?
"The feedback we got from our Learners was OFF-THE-CHARTS!," says our team!	Feedback is king. Success is not based on completing the process or *our* perceptions of the LX.

HOW WILL WE CREATE A FRANKLIN'S BBQ EXPERIENCE FOR OUR LCD SOLUTION?

If we want our Learners to truly understand our LCD solution in a way that they can work for them in their own context, the last thing they need is to only hear about it. It's not called Professional Listening, it's called Professional LEARNING, silly! They need an opportunity to actually LEARN our LCD solution, not just be told about it.

A study facilitated by the Gates Foundation called: "Teachers Know Best - Teachers' Views on Professional Development" found that leaders and teachers largely agree on what effective professional learning looks like: "relevant, hands-on, and sustained over time."

> So, what about you? How do you learn best?

Exercise: Let's press pause for a moment. Think of a powerful LX that you have had. This might not have happened in education: perhaps it was when you learned to surf or maybe when you learned a new music composition software and created your first song. What made that LX powerful? In the space below, fill in as many terms as you can to describe how *you* learn best.

If we truly want people to understand our LCD solutions, they will need to experience our LCD solutions in a way that truly acknowledges the findings in the Gates study and includes the elements of how our Learners learn best, just like the ones you described above in your top-drawer learning experience. Leap frogging great pedagogy is a bit like educational malpractice. The LCD Leader and the Design Team create the LX; it's in our hands. If we know what works for our Learners and we choose not to do it, then we can't blame them for the subsequent results, or lack there of. That's on us.

How do we create High-Impact Learning Experiences so we can truly proliferate solutions?

Remember: We will know our solution is successful when we actually observe our Learners achieving what we envisioned in the Illustrate Phase.

> To do this, we need to Crack the C.O.D.E. of High Impact LX.

CRACKING THE C.O.D.E. OF HIGH LX

CONNECTED - To research and to each of us

Time and money to create and execute immersive learning experiences is precious: if we don't have research (ethnography, data, and theory) that connect the initiative to improvement in student learning, schools and districts don't have the money or time to waste on it. Period. While learning about new solutions, initiatives or approaches to teaching and learning may not be the same as being immersed in an ice bath, changing classroom practices can represent a significant shock to the system. Learning is social (and can even be....gasp...FUN!). We must create a supportive, encouraging and laterally accountable environment (think training partner that kicks your tail off the couch to go for a run) to deal with obstacles that they will encounter along the way.

OBSERVABLE - The S.P.F. (Saying / Producing Factor)

Have you ever been at an education conference and noticed that the participants around you are sitting passively and listening to a witty and charming "edutainer" who shows pictures and YouTube clips while telling amusing anecdotes? Flip to the next conference you attend (perhaps when your mind is wandering as you watch your third YouTube video clip in the first ten minutes from yet another Edutainer) and well....rinse and repeat.

Cue: S.P.F. to protect us from the never-ending assault of passive learning.

What are Learners SAYING? What are Learners PRODUCING?

If you can't observe learning, you cannot guarantee it's happening!

What about thinking? Nope, that doesn't count either. Phrases like: "People were so engaged," or "I really made them think with that presentation!" or "That speaker had people eating out of the palm of their hand" mean very little unless there is EVIDENCE that resulted from it. Evidence is observable in the form of what we can observe our Learners producing during and as a result of the Learning Experience. The age-old proclamation of "If you get one good idea out of a conference, it was a good conference" doesn't fly anymore. With shrinking PD budgets and more demands on our time, the educational return on a $2000 investment needs to be better than ONE good idea. Are you kidding? You can get one good idea from a book that costs $12.95. You do the math...

Leaders of LCD and their Design Teams know they need to make the results of LX visible. This allows them to specifically and descriptively determine the level of comprehension of their Learners and determine whether to take additional steps to successfully proliferate.

CRACKING THE C.O.D.E. OF HIGH LX

DEVELOPMENTAL...it meets us where we are at

Would we ask a new swimmer to jump off of the high diving board? Or a novice skier to start down a double-black diamond run? Nope. So, imagine what it feels like for an educator to be asked to do Project Based Learning with their students when they have never done it before or to welcome observers into their classroom when they are used to being left on their own behind a closed classroom door. This can truly be a "double-black diamond" moment for many educators! Much like the students in our classrooms, we must always meet our Learners in our community where they are at to chart a course for their learning journey. Soviet psychologist Lev Vygotsky conceptualized the **Zone of Proximal Development** (ZPD) - the difference between what a learner can do without help and what he or she can do with help. LCD Leaders and their Design Teams need to be acutely aware of their Learners when designing LX in the Proliferate phase so they can scaffold activities to meet their Learners in their respective ZPD.

EMBEDDED...in what we do, in our context

LCD Leaders and their Design Teams know they must create Learning Experiences that mirror the day-to-day context of their Learners. If this sounds a bit like "meeting people where they are at," or the ZPD previously described, you're not far off. However, there is something else: a factor so important that it is truly shocking how often we leaders neglect to consider it. It's something we here at PLBC call ZPW: **the Zone of Proximal Workflow.** Learners are much more likely to grab onto new initiatives or LCD solutions and pull them into their day-to-day work (Zone 1) when it won't significantly add to their jam-packed workflows. Conversely, if a new initiative is so far away (Zone 3-4) from the Learner's Zone of Proximal Workflow, even if it is within their Zone of Proximal Development, they will be unlikely to get started.

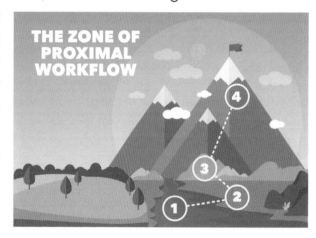

THE ZONE OF PROXIMAL WORKFLOW

It's a question of ability versus capacity. Our Learners may be ABLE to do it, but a saturated workflow could stand in the way. **They simply don't have the bandwidth.** As much as we may have fit, trained and experienced climbers who are ready to summit Mt. Everest, if they can't get time off from their day jobs, the summit will remain a pipe dream. How will we lighten the load (the *work*load)? How will we take something OFF their already-full-plates? If we don't to this, it's like offering a sumptuous apple pie *(baked with love)* to a guest who's already stuffed full of dinner. We're hurt that they don't even want to try it, but in all honesty they just can't take another bite.

CHANGING CHANGE

SHARE YOUR DRAFT CHANGE PROCESS

 TARGETED LX

Why choose this LX? Current perceptions of this LX?

FOCUSING QUESTION

Your "minute-to-get-it" call to action...

DESIGN TEAM

Who? Why them? How will you build cohesion?

▶ **APPRECIATE**

How will you build understanding and empathy about current state of LX?

▶ **ILLUSTRATE**

How will you craft a vision & set targets, while avoiding premature ideation?

LEARNER CENTERED DESIGN

APPRECIATE
ILLUSTRATE
IDEATE
ITERATE
PROLIFERATE

▶ **IDEATE**

How will you ignite creativity to generate tons of possible ideas?

▶ **ITERATE**

How will you try, test and improve ideas?

▶ **PROLIFERATE**

How will you determine the best way(s) to share your solution(s)?

GET HUNGRY FOR FEEDBACK

GALLERY WALK PROTOCOL

STEP 1 - Set Up: Hang posters and distribute sticky notes. (1-5 mins)

STEP 2 - Gallery Walk & Feedback: Silently record feedback on sticky notes using specific "I likes" and "I wonders." Give at least one "I like" and one "I wonder" per poster. (15-30 mins)

STEP 3 - Reflect: Categorize feedback, find trends, follow-up wherever you need more information and then use the feedback to make your work better. (5-30 mins)

What's the point of getting feedback if you don't change your idea?

SORT YOUR FEEDBACK

WARMS	COOLS	QUESTIONS

DETERMINE MODS & NEXT STEPS

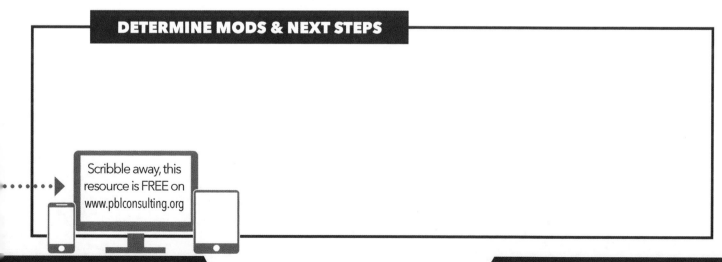

Scribble away, this resource is FREE on www.pblconsulting.org

CHANGING CHANGE

THE SIXTH "-ATE" - CELEBRATE

WHERE IS THE MISSING -ATE? CELEBRATE!

So there it is. The Proliferation Phase is complete. As an LCD Leader, you feel incredibly satisfied. It seems like a long time ago that you assembled your Design Team, a collection of "unusual suspects" with diverse skill sets that suited the challenge. Your team did their ethnography and sat "knee to knee" with your Learners and discovered surprising pain points in the current Learner Experience. Each of you has realized through the LCD process that your Learners weren't disinterested, or lazy, or whiny, grumpy, or uncaring - they were disempowered. Prior to the LCD process, your Learners might have had a voice that was interpreted as "resistance," but by walking miles and miles in their shoes, by working with them through illustrating a vision and by creating and testing ideas that you might not have thought were possible, you have realized this **resistance came from a genuine need for our Learners' voices to be heard and a need to know beyond a shadow of a doubt that their work makes a difference.**

In 2016, Professor John Hattie ranked collective teacher efficacy as the number ONE factor influencing student achievement. What is collective teacher efficacy? According to Tschannen-Moran and Barr (2004, p 190), it is the, **"collective self-perception that teachers in a given school make an educational difference to their students over and above the educational impact of their homes and communities."** In Hattie's work, collective efficacy has **more than double** the effect size of feedback and **more than triple the effect size** of socioeconomic status and student motivation! (Hattie, 2012) How does LCD help us tackle the clear priority of efficacy?

As an LCD Leader, you and your team have come to realize that the LCD Process is rigorous and when it's done well, it WORKS! It works even better to achieve solutions for our Learners then our shallow problem solving processes of the past (remember "solution-itis?") Doesn't it feel good when our hard work positively impacts our Learners? Each successful use of LCD creates yet another proof point that our work is actually positively impacting our Learners. So, over time, as these proof points add up, how do you think they will increase our educators' beliefs that their work can make a difference? Oh wait, that sounds like efficacy, right? *(Our belief that we can impact the results of our Learners.)* When we know that collective teacher efficacy is so positively connected to student achievement and we have a tool that could increase efficacy, then **shouldn't LCD be the heart pumping blood through our Learning Organizations?** LCD ought to be how we do things.

> "..schools that engage in collaborative inquiry develop a sense of collective efficacy that helps educators reconnect with their original point of passion: ensuring student success"
>
> -Langer (2005, p. 26)

CHANGING CHANGE USING LCD

Yes, it IS time to celebrate. And LCD Leaders know that the true celebration is not in celebrating a final product - there is no FINAL product... Remember? Schools-that-work have achieved **a homeostasis of continuous improvement**. Their constant *is change*. That's because the needs of our Learners will constantly evolve and, as LCD Leaders, we know that we have to continuously evolve with those needs by re-visiting the LX. The only way to re-visit the LX is through our ethnography in the Appreciate phase. We must go back to those Learners and appreciate where they are at and where they want to go with Learning Experiences. And the cycle continues... The LCD process begins again. And so it should. We should constantly be looking for the LX that surprises and delights in our schools every day. With the Learners that are in front of us every day: our students, our educators and our school community.

"So how about that celebration....?" You ask. Well, it comes not from a finished product, but from the fact that we have created exciting and unique approaches to the LX that are never "immovable stakes in the ground." Instead our celebration comes from the strong bonds that we have created with our Design Team and with our community through each phase of the LCD process. From that first meeting, to the interviews with our Learners, to talking to different people, to looking in unexpected places to find inspiration, to creating wacky and crazy ideas, to the unforgettable feeling of the sky-high "puke to excitement ratio" that we felt when we were testing and proliferating some of our ideas, to watching our Learners take them and make them even better. It's amazing how doing important work for our Learners takes everything full circle.

If we are truly LCD leaders, we know that the only constant in our schools, in our community and in our society is CHANGE. The right kind of change is continuous improvement using a process like LCD that connects, empowers and actually works. If we truly embrace change as something that is not only necessary, but something that can be EXCITING, that can BRING US TOGETHER and that can demonstrate that WE MAKE A DIFFERENCE, well...we will CHANGE the experience of CHANGE.

Congratulations, you will be CHANGING CHANGE using Learner-Centered Design to go **FROM** failed initiatives **TO** a change process that connects, empowers and actually works!

A BIT ABOUT THE AUTHORS

CALE BIRK is a District Head of Innovation in British Columbia, Canada and Senior Leadership Consultant for PBLC. In his 15 years as a high school administrator, Cale has lived through the challenges that come with implementing change at nearly every level of the school system. From the classroom to the boardroom, Cale has used numerous approaches to implement changes to pedagogy, practice, and policy to in order to improve teaching and learning in schools. Some of those change processes went smoothly, and some did not. Drawing on these experiences, Cale works with leaders on a daily basis to use practical strategies to re-imagine the process of change in their schools. Cale helps leaders to envision the development of every LX - class, faculty meeting, professional learning day, administrative meeting, Parent Advisory Council session and more - as an opportunity to build connections and empower improvement in our learning organizations and beyond.

Cale has worked with leaders in education and health care in Canada, the U.S. and in Asia to re-imagine the use of their existing resources and empower their personnel to co-design and implement engaging learning experiences for their organizations. He and his wife Lori live a quiet, relaxed, and peaceful life with their two young children, Paige and Kate. (Author's Note: If you look up the terms "quiet", "relaxed", and "peaceful" in the Birk household dictionary, they actually translate to "deafening", "chaotic", and "hilarious").

CHARITY ALLEN is a creative leader focused on innovation in education. She currently serves as President and CEO of PBLC, an independent consulting group empowering Deeper Learning. She has years of experience as a passionate educator, consultant, leadership coach and professional development designer and facilitator. She is slightly fanatical about Deeper Learning and stays focused on empowering powerful teaching and learning through Project-Based Learning, gamification, STEAM and more. She loves connecting with educators, inspiring creativity and vesting herself in the success of the team!

The breadth of her consulting work has been vast: six countries - the U.S., Qatar, the United Arab Emirates, Canada, Australia and India - nearly twenty states, over forty districts and well over one hundred different schools. She designs and delivers immersive professional learning experiences in both English and in French. She provides ongoing support to teachers in rural, suburban and deeply urban settings, including: Los Angeles Unified, Detroit, Chicago, New York, Dallas and in her home city of Seattle where you'll find Charity and her 13 year-old Nerd-tastic son John.

Throughout all of this work, Charity has been exposed to dozens of change initiatives, only to find many of them are failing... Upon closer look, that failure was predictable; they were designed to fail... She began changing change, only to find that we CAN achieve great things for kids, and for adults, in our organizations. Change matters and the experience of change matters. It can be pleasant, powerful and effective.

WE'D LOVE TO WORK WITH YOU!

WORKSHOP ONE

CONNECT & APPRECIATE

Let us model how to get started with LCD. Prior to arrving, we collaborate with you to target an LX, craft a focusing question and assemble a team.

During the full-day workshop we will connect your team and plan to do your I.N.T.E.L. for the Appreciate Phase.

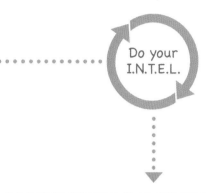

Do your I.N.T.E.L.

LCDX
The LCD Experience

WORKSHOP TWO (DAY 1)

ANALYZE & ILLUSTRATE

We come back together to analyze our I.N.T.E.L. as well as come to a deeper understanding and appreciation of the problem. Then, we illustrate our goals and targets in this full-day workshop.

WORKSHOP TWO (DAY 2)

IDEATE POSSIBILITIES

On day two, we model unleashing the creative potential of your team using a variety of fun, powerful and effective protocols, techniques and strategies to generate dozens of ideas. Then, we plan to iterate your best ideas.

WORKSHOP THREE

REFLECT & PROLIFERATE

We return to guide reflections on the best solutions bubbling to the surface of the Iteration Phase. We support your team in co-determining the best ways to design High Impact LX that cracks the C.O.D.E. for proliferating solutions to your Learners...and beyond.

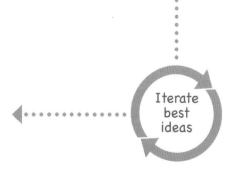

Iterate best ideas

PBLC PROFESSIONAL LEARNING MENU

INTRO TO PBL

Clarifies the what: What is PBL, what is it not?

Illustrates the how: Apply an intuitive design process for high quality PBL through which participants *actually* develop an original project.

PROJECT SLICES

Learn PBL, by experiencing PBL.

OPTION 1: BIOMIMICRY DESIGNS

Use Design Thinking to ideate a solution that is inspired by nature and that helps humans with an everyday problem.

OPTION 2: MECHANIZED MASTERPIECES

Art, engineering and language arts are remixed together as participants explore an essential question. Participants experience Design Thinking first-hand as a process to brainstorm, conceptualize and iterate a product to publicly exhibit.

WORKSHOPS FOR DEEPER LEARNING

Each of these 1-3 day workshops creates opportunities for teachers to experience the topics and to develop materials they can use in their classrooms beyond the workshop to advance Deeper Learning.

1. Pathways to Personalization
2. Advancing Critical Thinking
3. Cultivating Collaboration
4. Producing Powerful Presenters
5. Teaching Creativity & Innovation
6. From Consumer to Producer
7. Decoding Differentiated Instruction
8. Curriculum Mapping & Classroom Branding
9. Cultivating Culture
10. Balanced Assessment
11. Automated "Making" (*Arduino*)
12. Taking your class 3D (*3D Printing*)

PBL

DEEPER LEARNING

PD

FOR LEADERS: LCD

COACHING

WORKSHOPS FOR LEADERS

LEARNER-CENTERED DESIGN

LCD is a process for leaders to facilitate change and improvement in their schools.

Jump start "the how" as participants prepare to lead LCD *well* in our workshops on LCD through which leaders experience the process and prepare to lead it themselves. Get ready and gear up to accelerate your improvement work towards powerful teaching and learning in our schools!

SUSTAINED SUPPORT

Success with Deeper Learning isn't achieved overnight. Deepening practice requires support.

PBL Consulting is committed to providing ongoing, customized coaching to advance growth in practice for each of the schools, districts and organizations we serve.

DIGITAL AND FACE-TO-FACE COACHING OPTIONS AVAILABLE

WORKS CITED

A Game-Changing Home Product Swiffer - Continuum." 2012. 27 May. 2016 Retrieved February 10, 2017, from http://continuuminnovation.com/work/swiffer/.

Anderson, D.L. (2012). Organization Development: The Process of Leading Organizational Change. Los Angeles. Sage.

Barry, Keith (2008, November 14). Study Shows Drivers Feel Free to Ignore Speed Limits. Wired Magazine, p. 1-3. Retrieved from https://www.wired.com/2008/11/the-boy-who-cri/.

Donohoo, Jenni (2016, July 13). Fostering Collective Teacher Efficacy: Three Enabling Conditions [Web log post]. Retrieved March 9, 2017, from http://corwin-connect.com/2016/07/fostering-collective-teacher-efficacy-three-enabling-conditions/.

Dyer, Jeffrey H. (2009, December 1). The Innovator's DNA. Harvard Business Review, p. 1-9. Retrieved from www.hbr.org.

Hattie, J. (2012). Visible learning for teachers: Maximizing impact on learning. Routledge. New York, NY.

Langer, G., & Colton, A. (2005). Looking at Student Work. Education Leadership, 62(5), p. 22-26.

Only Connect!: A new paradigm for learning innovation in the 21st century", Occasional Paper No. 112, Centre for Strategic Education.

Reeves, D. B. (2006). The learning leader: how to focus school improvement for better results. Alexandria, VA: Association for Supervision and Curriculum Development.

Senge, P., Kleiner, A. Roberts, C., Ross, R., Roth, G., & Smith, B. (1999). *The dance of change*. New York: Doubleday.

Starbucks. (2017). Retrieved February 16, 2017, from https://www.starbucks.com/about-us/company-information/mission-statement.

The Definition of User Experience (UX) - Nielsen Norman Group." 2015. 26 May. 2016 <https://www.nngroup.com/articles/definition-user-experience/>

Vullings, Ramon (2015). Not Invented Here: Cross-industry Innovation.: BIS Publishers.

Made in the USA
Columbia, SC
15 December 2017